Hurricane Harvey

A Storm Like No Other

By Members of the
Greater League City Community

TotalRecall Publications, Inc.
1103 Middlecreek
Friendswood, Texas 77546
281-992-3131 281-Tel
www.totalrecallpress.com

Copyright © 2023 by City of League City, Texas
Project Leads: Joanne Turner and Caris Brown, The Helen Hall Library
Editor: Chris O'Shea Roper

ISBN: 978-1-64883-187-4
UPC: 6-43977-41874-6

Library of Congress Control Number: 2023934292

FIRST EDITION
1   2   3   4   5   6   7   8   9   10

Dedication

Hurricane Harvey: A Storm Like No Other is dedicated to the people of the greater League City area who struggled with the onslaught of the major storm event that was Hurricane Harvey. The citizens of this area worked together to overcome and repair the physical damage to their homes and reached out to help each other in the aftermath of this historic event.

Acknowledgements

The purpose of this book is to help preserve the community memory of the catastrophic Hurricane Harvey event and its impact on the people of League City and the surrounding area. The project has successfully been accomplished due to the contributions of the following:

- o All of the community residents, families and neighbors who shared their stories of hardship and hard work, of compassion and generosity, of loss and growth, of faith and resilience. This book is their story.

- o Joanne Turner of the Helen Hall Library staff who is the vision behind this memorial project.

- o Members of the Marketing and Publishing (MAP) Group of the League City Library who were driving forces behind completion of the project, particularly those who worked to compile the stories: Cathy Chapman, Jackie May, Roberta Shepherd and Patricia Vance.

- o The Friends of the Helen Hall Library, who have generously underwritten the project.

- o All of the League City officials who graciously consented to be interviewed for their stories.

- o The editor (Chris O'Shea Roper) and printer (Bruce Moran of TotalRecall Publications) who generously donated their time and effort to bring this book to life.

Thank you all.

Credits

Front Cover Photo:
    League City officers Aaron McGaughey and Matt Strachan and Lt. Shawn Murray conducted search-and-rescue operations in fast-moving and deep water during Hurricane Harvey. Photo courtesy of League City Police Department

Back Cover Photo:
    The MRAP was an indispensable vehicle for rescuing people flooded out of their homes. Photo courtesy of League City Police Department

Contributing Writers:
    Community residents and members of the Marketing and Publishing Group of the Helen Hall Library

Stories Compiled by:
    Roberta Shepherd, Jackie May, Patricia Vance, Cathy Chapman and other MAP members

Table of Contents

I
A Unifying Faith in Heroism
by Pat Hallisey, Mayor

Hurricane Harvey hit the latter part of 2017 and the aftermath rolled over into 2018. Most of what I remember about the storm happened in October of 2017.

I was aware of the storm about a week prior to Harvey hitting the city. I watched it on TV like most people. Ryan Edghill was our Emergency Management Coordinator, and I was in communication with him about what the storm was doing. Most tropical storms come, blow through and are gone, but not this one.

I watched it from the Emergency Operation Center (EOC), left there at 10:00 the evening before the full storm hit and went to bed around 11:00 pm. I knew there was going to be a lot of rain, but I never dreamt it was going to be the kind of rain that it was.

At 5:00 in the morning, my wife woke me, and I looked out the kitchen window. It looked like a lake. We live 300 to 400 yards from Clear Creek. We are up high, and the house had never flooded before. After looking out the kitchen window, I immediately ran to the front door. When I opened it, I saw the water had come all the way from the creek and was about five feet from coming in the house.

I started calling my neighbors. One of my oldest friends in the county was my first call. Judge Garner lived across the street and down a bit, his house about 200 yards from the creek. He said he already had water in his house, and he and his wife were getting out. Their daughter was going to pick them up at the front of the neighborhood. I told him to come by our house to wait and get dry. We had coffee for him.

Now, Judge Garner is around 6'3", and when he came out of his house, the water was up to his shoulders. His poor wife was hanging onto him so she wouldn't be swept away. They made it to our house and had coffee and went on to their next stop up the street, where his daughter was able to pick them up. They ended up with nine or ten feet of water in their house by the next night. It was a bad deal.

It was pretty obvious at this point that this storm was more than I had ever seen before. I had been through Claudette in 1979, but I had never seen anything quite like this. And I knew this was just the beginning.

Shortly after Judge Garner left, my wife Janice and I went around the corner to see another neighbor, the Jacobsons. We sat there and saw all kinds of people in canoes and other stuff going up and down the street.

Ultimately, Janice's sister and brother-in-law came and picked us up because we couldn't get our cars out of the driveway. They took us to their home in Tuscan Lakes to spend the night. The day after the storm hit, we waded back into our neighborhood and saw that we had two to three feet of water in our house. We didn't have nine feet as others had, but it still hit us pretty hard. We went into recovery mode immediately. I called the insurance company, FEMA and everybody else. We stayed at Janice's sister's house because we couldn't move back into our house.

Then, suddenly, I got a call from Ryan Edghill at the Emergency Operations Center, saying that so many neighborhoods had been impacted and calling it a catastrophe.

Officers Jason Kifer and Matt Maggiolino walk through
knee-deep water to aid residents of a flooded neighborhood
Photo courtesy of League City Police Department

It took a couple of days for the water to subside and when it did, I talked to the newspapers. I took them through my neighborhood and showed them other neighborhoods so that they could talk to people who, by all accounts, had lost everything. The newspapers did a series of stories on those people.

At that point, we knew of only one death in town. One gentleman in Bay Colony had been swept up in the current. That was bad enough, that we had one fatality, but people needed to pay attention so there weren't more. There were currents in the water, snakes coming out of their holes, and other stuff to watch out for. Dickinson Bayou had come up and hit Bay Colony. Clear Creek got everything on this side. It was several days before the water subsided. People were just beside themselves. What were we going to do?

After working with my wife to get our personal bearings, the first thing someone in my position needs to do in an emergency like this is to reassure people that it is going to be okay. I wasn't on Facebook Live at that time, but I knew other people who were. So someone came in and videotaped me every morning. I sent out positive messages throughout the neighborhoods that, in fact, this trouble would pass. The water would subside, help was coming, and we would be okay. I did this for at least seven days, I think.

Jason Kifer and Matt Maggiolino help a resident after driving her through high water in the Police MRAP (Mine-resistant Ambush Protected vehicle)
Photo courtesy of League City Police Department

I checked with the Police Department, Fire Department, Emergency Management team, and everybody else involved. We were all communicating on cell phones. We also needed to make sure FEMA knew of our situation. We needed to get our emergency declaration drafted. John Baumgartner, City Manager, took care of all that. His side of town didn't have nearly as much damage as mine, so he was a lot more mobile and could get around to get things done.

It was a sobering experience. By the end of the first week, I realized that I needed more than just going on Facebook Live. I also needed to make personal appearances in these neighborhoods. A woman over here at Victory Lakes kept calling me that the school district wouldn't open the school as a refuge. I called Greg Smith and got that school opened in five minutes. We had opened shelters at Hometown Heroes Park, Victory Lakes Intermediate School, Clear Creek Intermediate School, and the Baptist Church on the west side. I went to each one of them to check on people. I saw that most of the churches in the city were coming out and feeding people, and it gave me a great appreciation for the wonderful people in this town.

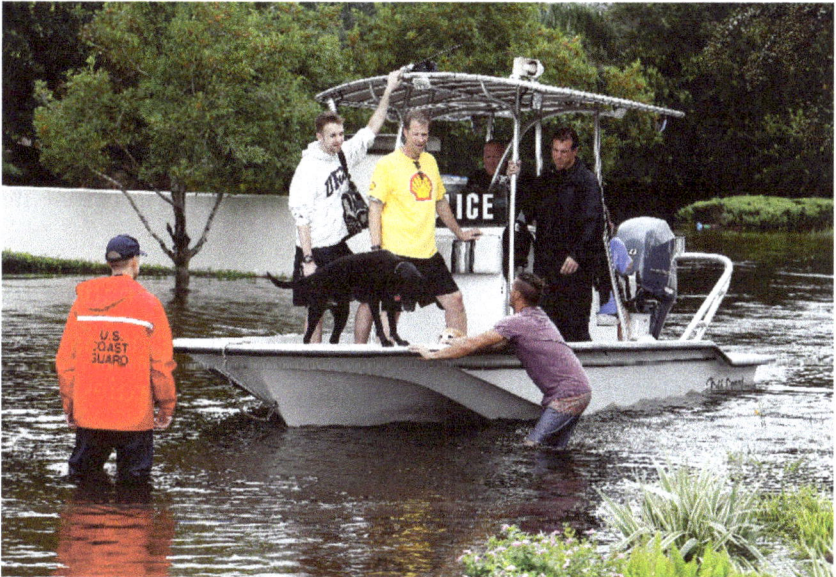

Officer Matt Strahan picks up stranded residents
in a Police boat to take them to safety.
Photo courtesy of League City Police Department

The other thing I observed was neighbors helping neighbors who were devastated by flood waters. I had never before seen the community come together like they did. I told people in my speeches for several years afterward that it was a bittersweet experience: Bitter because of all the devastation that had been done; sweet because we saw the good in people. We saw the good in our churches. I got all excited about the faith community here because they were demonstrating what I always had hoped would happen. As part of the recovery effort, I started a ministerial line of communication, and it still goes on to this day.

At the City offices, we were trying to figure out what to do. The first question out the door was how to feed people? How do we clothe them? Then how do we help them have good hope for tomorrow? Ryan Dennard, who had been a county commissioner but retired here to League City, came to see me and offered help. He said he had contacts with Kroger's corporate offices. I told him what we would really like to do with Kroger's corporate offices was open a distribution center. First to take in donations, which we also did on Facebook, and then to distribute the whole array of what people needed: food, clothing, dog food, water, whatever people needed. We were novices at this.

We had probably 90 communities across this nation that poured donations into our local entities to meet the needs of our people. We asked for volunteers and gathered the hardiest bunch anyone could ask for. They worked for the next five or six weeks from eight in the morning till ten o'clock at night. We broadcast on Facebook until we got everything up and running, letting people know that help was available and all they had to do was come down and we would help them – help them get food, shelter, cleaning supplies -- whatever they needed to get their houses back in order.

At the same time Greg Gripon, a member of the City Council, had taken on Hometown Heroes Park more than any of the others. His whole family helped out there. He opened that place up to everybody without a home or a place to live. The gyms were full of people, and he made sure they had food.

Officer Clayton Shaw helps a small child
through her flooded neighborhood.
Photo courtesy of League City Police Department

I went out to the Baptist Church on the east side of town and saw everyone in the Knights of Columbus chapter from my church cooking food for people.

Joel McMahon asked what he could do to help. He had recently left League City United Methodist Church but was out there making sure people had food. In fact, the first people evacuated from my neighborhood were brought out by League

City United Methodist Church. One of the parishioners out there even came by and checked all our sheetrock and told us what we needed to do to fix it.

All of this work went on for probably a month. We were trying to get back on our feet. We were trying to be understanding. We talked about doing away with water bills for people. We didn't want to hit them when their houses were destroyed. We wanted them to have as much of their own disposable income as possible to use for fixing up their homes.

Meanwhile, Greg Gripon and I were loading up trailers and going out to the neighborhoods. The first one I went to was Bay Ridge. This story is kind of funny now, although it wasn't at the time. Bay Ridge was totally devastated, and they had just barely gotten the water out. I walked out to about 250 people who were looking for someone to be mad at, and they didn't care who it was. So there I was, like a goofball, telling them we didn't know why they flooded. I tried talking to them about the 1979 flood because I had spent my time then running up and down getting people out of that flood. I had been an employee of the City then.

But they didn't care. They didn't want to hear that. They just wanted to be mad. I understood that. It wasn't my place to reassure them after they had lost everything. I told them that day that we were going to stay on this issue until we had a solution.

Gum Bayou had to be repaired all the way to Dickinson Bayou. The underground utilities out there that took the rain run-off, the neighborhood, and everything had to be fixed. And, here we are today, finishing up almost $15,000,000 worth of work in Bay Ridge alone.

While we were trying to prop everybody up, we began to see that this was bigger than any of us could handle in short order.

So even when people were still mucking out houses, we started looking at a bond issue. I hate to say it like this, but nothing will encourage people to support a bond issue when they are in the middle of a catastrophe. So we started plotting and scheming.

The bond issues for the previous four years had all failed. I made the comment to the City Council that we couldn't do things the same old way this time. Normally, we would post a bond issue on what we intended to do. We wanted property tax to pay for it, but we live in an ultra-conservative community. Our residents will go to their deaths fighting property tax increases, and we knew that.

The Council said, "What do we do?"

I said, "Let's take a look at sales tax."

A sales tax is not a property tax, but rather a tax paid by people who go to the store and buy things. The big part of a sales tax (or any time you ask a community for money) is that you have to tell them what it is for. That had been the problem with the previous four bond issues.

I told them to put the package together, identify where the lead projects would be, and in which neighborhoods. I personally went out to sell that program. I told every Council member that they had to be right there with me. We could not have one person say, "No, we don't want to do this." You have to see the need and the validity of going out and selling the whole package to the community, which has always been my big deal.

So we did. We hit the road. We talked to all 95 homeowner groups. We pled our case. We reminded them of what had happened. And in 2018, it passed by 65-70% on all issues. It worked out well. Now we needed to hurry up and get it all done for people.

At the same time we were planning for the future, we were still rescuing people and property. The EMC (Emergency Management Coordinator) was an integral part of the Fire Department and Police Department rescues. Water rescue was our biggest problem. We didn't have boats to speak of; we had trucks.

Officer Clayton Shaw pulls a rescue boat through
waist-deep water and strong currents.
Photo courtesy of League City Police Department

The police had a couple of oversized vehicles to pick up people. But we needed help.

The Public Works Department flew into action. They brought all their trucks in and started carting people out of neighborhoods. I saw Jody Hooks, the Director of Public Works, sitting in the front of a dump truck and the 80-year-old neighbors down the street from me sitting in the back of the truck in chairs.

I'm thinking, "Who thought that up and how did you get them up there?" They were quick to tell me that they had a ladder for them to crawl up.

Tommy Cones, the Assistant Fire Chief, and the rest of the Fire Department team were out in Bay Colony with the Police pulling people out of their homes and getting them to safety. The institution of government worked at a very high level to protect the people of League City. You could not have asked the institution of government to do anything more.

When I went out to Hometown Heroes, there were 500 people with cots in the gym, including my neighbors who lived at the end of our street, closer to the creek. I tried to reassure them and others in the gym that it was going to be okay. It didn't look good then, but things were going to pass; it would be okay.

All the schools and churches were taking in the displaced citizens. The Lions' Club and all the not-for-profits jumped to feed people while they were hung up. It was terrific.

I thought, "Where were these people to go? They had nothing. Their cars were underwater. Their houses were underwater."

Their children had to eat, and the community came to their rescue. It was the most marvelous thing I had ever seen in this city. I had been through the flood in 1979. I carted people out of the back of Bay Ridge. It was bad then, but I did not see neighbors helping neighbors as I saw during Hurricane Harvey. I didn't see the churches coming out and doing everything they could do to put people in a safe environment where they could sleep, eat, and get back on their feet. I will always have a special place in my heart for the faith community in this town after Harvey.

There was a lady who lived down the street from me who was stranded in her house on the second floor. She popped the window open and started screaming because she was scared. She was afraid the water was going to carry her away. The guys across the street heard her crying and waded through the water and carted her out of there. Her name was Frankie Blansit. Her husband Max had just passed away, so everyone knew she was alone. She was stuck and had no place to go. They helped her get out. They walked her across the street and helped her into a dump truck when it came by. They got her out of the neighborhood. She went to Pasadena and still hasn't come back to the house.

Officer Jason Kifer assists a stranded resident
into the MRAP for transport to safety.
Photo courtesy of League City Police Department

Down the street from our house, there was a man named Tony who was 103. He was a friend of our son and daughter-in-law, and he went to church with us. His wife had passed away a year or so before. His son-in-law called me asking if I had seen him. Now, keep in mind Tony was 103.

I said, "No I haven't seen Tony. I know he's at the house. What's happening?"

He said, "I'm worried about him. He has a caretaker in the house. I heard that all night he had been walking up and down the hall, rattling her doorknob and screaming, 'Are you sure you don't want to be my girlfriend anymore?'"

Apparently, she was petrified and wouldn't come out of the room. He and I had a laugh and observed that the body may go but the brain never quits.

The neighbors started to bring food to Tony because he couldn't go anywhere. Ultimately, they put him in a boat, carted him out of there and got him to his daughter's house. He passed away a year later.

I heard stories of people scared to death that their children would be caught up in the water. Then neighbors came to help them. The police came to help. Firemen came to help. In people's most vulnerable moments, others were there to help.

Folks all around my neighborhood experienced the same thing. Some people had four or five feet of water in their houses. In the lower part of the neighborhood, which is down my street where it turns into a curve, they had nine, ten, and eleven feet of water. The creek really came up and people lost everything. The old part of the neighborhood on Aggie Lane and Audubon had ten to eleven feet, just like they did in Hurricane Claudette. It was a bad time for people.

These stories are a dime a dozen. Go to Bay Colony, Newport, Clear Creek Village, Countryside, The Park on the west side, and Bay Ridge. All these communities had stories.

Now they are all rebuilt. People are back in their homes. The aftermath of Harvey was an amazing moment for the history of this town. I don't know who else will remember it like that, but I certainly do.

It was my biggest dream that something would happen while I was mayor –not a catastrophe – but something that would bind this community together. We had become so fragmented. We didn't like taxes. We didn't like the people in office. We didn't openly fight back and forth, but we didn't have a "unifying faith in heroism," before Harvey. But here it was, happening right in front of us.

FEMA was in here pretty quick, trying to get people back on their feet. We couldn't have asked for a better deal. We had the Governor come down and see what was going on here. He came and toured the community. The Lieutenant Governor came, and congressmen were in and out quite a bit. All our state legislators were here quite often. County judges and the Commissioner came by to help. So we did a lot of escorting them around to let them see how bad it was. It was bad!

I think there were a lot of us that assumed this was going to pass, that we were going to have a better day soon. But at the time, I wasn't sure we really believed it as much as we were just trying to calm people down because that is what you have to do. You have to send them a message that you care. You send the message of hope because hope springs eternal.

Here is another funny story. Well, not funny exactly, but a wonderful story and testament to this community.

By the end of the first month, around the first of October, I had been out every day. I was up late, wasn't eating well, and wasn't getting enough sleep. I got up the morning of October 9th, totally rung out. To add to that, the creek behind our backyard had washed over our pool and yard, plus we had a garage apartment where our daughter had lived which got four feet of water.

I told my wife that morning, "Look, I know I've been busy and haven't had time to fiddle with our own stuff, but I'm coming home this afternoon." I intended to start working on the pool and tearing out sheetrock. I went out in the morning and did my thing, and around two o'clock in the afternoon, I came home incredibly tired. So I laid down in the backyard.

My daughter, who was there at that time, came and asked, "Dad, what's the matter?"

I said, "I'm just tired. I'm going to take a little nap here. I'll be just fine in a bit."

She left me snoozing on the edge of the pool. She came back 45 minutes later and said, "Are you okay?"

I sat up and she took a look at me. She told me later that my eyes rolled to the back of my head. She panicked and ran to call my wife, who was out doing some group thing somewhere.

At that time, we were living in an RV in the driveway. My daughter got me into the RV and I just started throwing up like crazy. It was the worst that I had ever experienced.

When my wife got there, she said, "You look terrible. We have to get you to a hospital."

I said, "Take me to UTMB Clear Lake." It seemed like the right thing to do.

I got there but, to tell you the truth, I don't really know what happened then. I've been told.

I am diabetic and, apparently, I had experienced two heart attacks in the backyard and had 100% blockage in both legs. My whole system had been stressed and all the heaving that I had been doing in the RV was apparently when I was having the heart attacks, although it has never been confirmed.

As I was being checked into the Emergency Room, who do I meet but a guy I had known 40 years ago in town. He was an EMS through our Volunteer Fire Department, and he took good care of me.

Apparently, the doctors there at UTMB wanted to take both my legs off. My wife was just furious: That wasn't going to happen.

Two women from Memorial Herman, Ashlea Quinonez who is a personal friend of ours and does government relations, and Rebecca Lilley, who is a physician at League City Southeast Memorial, stuck themselves between us and the doctors. Rebecca got on the phone and called Life Flight because they said I couldn't be moved by ambulance. I was just too unstable.

The next morning, they put me on Life Flight and took me to Memorial Herman downtown. That opened up a whole bunch of new people to deal with. Of course, I was not awake. I didn't really know what was going on by the time I got to Memorial Herman, but those doctors up there are first class. We became advocates for Memorial Herman long before they built the center over here in town because of their attention to detail. Their care is first class.

I did not wake up for 12 days. My wife says that is not so but that is my recollection. During that time, I had some dreams that would raise the hair on the back of anyone's neck. Through that time, it was touch-and-go for me.

When I finally did wake up, whenever that was, the first thing that I remembered was somebody talking about an amputation, but I wasn't sure. So I started wiggling the toes on my right foot and I could see the sheet moving. I started to wiggle the toes on my left foot. I could feel them moving but the sheet wasn't moving. I lifted the sheet and could see what had happened.

Right on the spot, I prayed, "Lord, I don't know what happened to me but please don't make me bitter about this. I'm going to keep a smile on my face every day." He has answered that!

About that time my daughter, who was 30 at that time, walked through the door and said, "I guess you are mad at me?"

I said, "Mad at you? Why would I be mad at you?"

She said, "Mom was a basket case. The doctors kept saying to take two legs. Mom held out saying 'No, just one leg.' Finally, the doctors came to me and said, 'We will take one leg, but we have to do it right now. If he doesn't wake up tomorrow morning because we didn't do enough for him, that will be on you all. You always told us life comes first and everything else is manageable.'"

After hearing this, I laid there scratching my head and thinking about my daughter, "You don't ever listen to me about anything, and at the most opportune time, that is what you remember."

I told her, "Of course, I'm not mad at you. I'm proud of you. Great job."

We are still best friends with Rebecca and Ashlea. There's not much I wouldn't do for them. In the most difficult time, Rebecca had the presence of mind to say, "We have to get him out of this hospital. He needs to be where the experts are, and that's at Memorial Herman."

The next thing I know, they are pushing me to get out to TIRR for outpatient rehabilitation. I'm not one for hanging around, but there was a lot I had to do in the hospital before I could go to TIRR. I didn't even know how to sit up. I had to think about that for a minute. Without a leg, my balance was off. And I had to figure out how to get back to work. So I went through the entire process.

I now accepted the fact that I was done with my part in the distribution center. The City had to take care of that, and they did. John Baumgartner, City Manager, did a great job making sure that it kept going and the volunteers were happy. Everything that I had been working on was pretty much continued, which is a testimony to the institution and caliber of the people we have. Without your people, you are just never anything. No one person does anything alone.

I think everything went well with the city's recovery. It was slow but methodical. We got FEMA helping in here quickly so people could start to rebuild their houses. BP from Texas City showed up with an $85,000 donation for us to buy boats. D.R. Horton, who is a contractor building houses in this town, brought in $75,000 to take care of the needs around town. We applied for grant money. John started pushing people to get things done. The city employees got right back to what they are good at, identifying needs and finding solutions to those needs. I could not be prouder of all the people who work here.

Just to follow up on my personal situation: While I was in the hospital, my wife was there with me from morning to midnight. My daughter was staying at one of her friends' houses and at our house. Suddenly two people in town, Tommy Cones, who is the Fire Marshall, and Deborah Bly, who owns a real estate company, took it upon themselves to step up to the plate and get our house back in order before I got out of the hospital. They opened a donation website and, in the end, probably raised $25,000. Everything was new in the house by the time I got home.

Deborah and Tommy also raised money throughout the community, somewhere around $60,000-70,000 to get our house handicap accessible. They worked morning, noon and night.

They made a list of things that had to change. They put handicap stuff in the shower so I could get in and out. In the bathroom, I now have all kinds of things I can pull myself up on.

Even the Fire Department trucks struggled
to get through the high water.
Photo courtesy of the City of League City

They had ramps installed at the front and back doors. They added concrete behind the garage to our storeroom so I could get back there in a wheelchair. The whole house is now ADA compliant.

Cervelle Homes came and laid concrete. Nick Albeba, who owns the Shell gas station up here and also builds, had his people put tile floors in for us. All the old wood floors were out in the front yard.

The whole community participated in getting us back on our feet. We are indebted for the rest of our lives to all those people who did so much for us. I tell people now that anything I do for League City is repayment for all of what League City has done for me.

It's easy to take a long view back to the storm now and how League City responded to the catastrophe. My first job in government was here in League City in 1975. I was an employee here until 1980. I then went to the County, but I still love League City today. This town has the warmest people anywhere. Yes, we have a history of nasty politics, but what small town doesn't? I get mad at people sometimes for being goofy, I don't like talking about pigs and all that stuff. But you just get through all that. We have bigger issues to deal with.

The warmth of this community to take in people who are down on their luck is just a miracle. I didn't see it anywhere else. I had contacts in every city, and I never saw it as I saw it here. So I'm very proud of League City.

The first thing I did when I got back on my feet, was get all the preachers in here. I told them all, "I have a planning committee, so if you are looking to expand your church or rebuild your church, or whatever you want to do, come in and we will put all of the current plans on a disk drive for you. You can take a look at where the city is growing. If you want to move in that direction, we're here. Any questions you want to ask us, or anything we can do to help you rebuild on a solid foundation in this town, we are here." We are still meeting with the church leaders to this day.

The generosity of people outside of this community and across the country is amazing. There were probably 90 tractor-trailer trucks that brought us supplies from California, Oklahoma, the Midwest, the Northeast, the Eastern seaboard and Florida, along with Louisiana. All of the volunteers unloaded all of those trucks. They brought it all into the distribution center and it all went out to the people of this community. But we didn't just limit it to people in this community because people in Dickinson and other areas were hurting, too. If you start to do that, you ruffle up feathers.

I heard someone comment, "Oh, this is just for League City."

And my response was a strong, "No! No, it's not."

Our hearts have to be big enough to recognize we aren't the only ones hurting. We had people coming from Houston, Pasadena and Beaumont for help, but we didn't care. If someone is hurting, you open the doors. That is what good Christians do. That is what good people do.

All across the board, we helped people. Responding in the way we did was probably our proudest moment. We now have a blueprint for anyone who faces a catastrophe in the future.

I learned from the great storm of 1900 in Galveston that everybody came to Galveston's defense. That storm killed around 10,000 people. They would never have rebuilt without Houston and all the rest of the mainland coming to their defense. Those are life lessons I learned along the way. I tried to quell these folks down when somebody said, "This is just for League City." We solved that pretty quickly -- and diplomatically. Yes, someone may have gotten offended but, in the end, they were happy. Of course, we preferred League City residents, then Galveston County, then the world, but we didn't turn anyone down. People were hurting.

I say that we should learn from what happens. If you open your heart to people, at the end of the day, the character of the community comes through. I'm a long-time believer that, when something happens to friends in life, you have to be there. When things are at their worst, you come to their defense because that is how you make good friends. You know we can do silly things sometimes, but I don't take much abuse from the community. Maybe a couple of times, but not much, and that's probably because I extend myself.

I think after the storm, I gave 150 to 200 speeches a year for a while, all about what we did. I tried to imprint it into people's minds in this town because I didn't want them to ever forget how generous people were to us. When we see people around the country that are hurting, it's our obligation to look at them and say, "What can we do to help?"

We had several City Council members go to Louisiana when they were flooding and take food and supplies to them just like people had done for us.

Paying it forward is a big part of life. You can't just take, say thank you and goodbye. You have to be prepared for the next time. When people are down on their luck and you are there to help them, people will always remember.

Your friends are the ones who come to your rescue when times are tough. When you are looking out over a bleak horizon, your friends will be there. Never forget who came to your defense in those difficult times. I have always tried to remember that. I was told that almost 50 years ago by one of my earliest mentors in government, and I still feel the same way. We look at these friends as our heroes, the ones who come to our rescue when times are tough.

In my eight years of being Mayor of League City, between this time and the first time, I realized that it is your friends who come to your rescue when times are really tough. And I believe that there is a unifying faith in that heroism.

II
Harvey Came in Like a Thief in the Night
by Gary D. Ratliff, Chief of Police

When Hurricane Harvey hit, I had been working here for 32 years and was Assistant Chief of Police. I was born and raised in this area and had been through a lot of storms. I remember the '79 flood. There was major flooding back then, but it was nothing like the levels we saw with Harvey.

Then, in 1983, we had Alicia, which caused some flooding. In 1991, Allison came in but didn't have the same impact as the others. That storm hit mostly in Brazoria County and up into Houston.

We have had several times throughout those years when we had high levels of water, but we never had any idea of what was going to befall us with Harvey. Of course, there is always a concern with hurricanes pushing water in with the storm surge, but not that level of rainfall.

During those years, we had developed plans for what to do in case of different storms. But we had no idea of the ramifications that would come from this storm. Nobody had any indication of how much water was coming and how badly it would impact everyone.

I knew the week before Harvey hit that there was a storm brewing out in the Gulf of Mexico, south of the Corpus Christi area. I met with our Emergency Management Coordinator (EMC) and had ongoing conversations with state and local officials throughout that week about the storm. Nobody was all that concerned. We thought we had a Category Two storm coming.

We look at a Category Two as a potential for some rain and a need for heightened awareness. But none of us believed that this storm would be anything to be all that worried about.

Officer Matt Maggiolino overlooks Harvey's widespread flooding from the back of the MRAP during the storm. Everyone was surprised by the level of flooding and storm damage that occurred.
Photo courtesy of League City Police Department

We have a Hurricane Activation Plan that goes into effect any time we are within 12 hours of landfall of a storm. We activate our teams and get everyone ready. All employees who are considered essential personnel come in with at least three days of clothing and other essentials that they might need. We work 12-hour shifts until the storm passes. Typically, it is the aftermath that we deal with, not the onslaught. On June 1 of each year, we notify everyone that we are in hurricane season and to be ready in case we might be activated.

This might sound crazy, but for the most part, I really enjoy our hurricane activations, because it's a time we get all of our teams together in one place. It is a time for our employees to come together as a team to respond to the needs of the community. We have a real sense of camaraderie. Before Ike, for example, we had a 12-hour notice. Everybody unloaded their refrigerators and brought their food up here and we had a big cook-out and plenty of food as we waited for the storm to roll in. Everybody already had their assignments, shifts and beats. In that case, we just rolled into our normal routine.

I like most of the storms, but not Harvey. Not one bit. It was terrible. But no matter what happens or takes place in the course of our response, our officers go over and above every time. There was no difference in this case. They do what they have to do at that moment to help folks get through it.

I think we have close to 185 people employed in this building. We pretty much felt like we could take in all our essential personnel. That's not including the Records Department and alternate positions and that sort of personnel, but we had quite a few folks here. When we start planning for a hurricane, we also think about who else would be good to have in place in the building, like Texas/New Mexico Power or whoever. That way, they are already here and can help us to be first back online, in the middle or after the storm.

Typically, with storms, we have our activation plan in place before the storm rolls in. All our people would be here, and notifications would be sent out to our citizens to evacuate, if need be.

This just wasn't that kind of storm. We are not a shelter-in-place type of community. Typically, we send people out of town.

The reason for this is because, at the height of a storm when the wind gets to be a certain strength, I pull my people off the streets. It is just too dangerous to be driving in high winds. If an officer was to get out of his vehicle in a gust of 37 mph, it would fold the car door back. Then the officer could be injured and we would lose that unit and officer for the entire storm. In that case, we call all of our units in until the wind dies down. Then we go out and do recovery and try to get the city rolling again.

With most storms, we have evacuation plans. When the danger gets to a certain level, we want to get people out of harm's way. We will send our evacuation order to the Mayor and he will approve it. This is usually done in concert with the County and State's recommendations. We also evacuate our jail any time we have a storm coming in. The prisoners are either released on a personal recognizance bond or sent to the county or whatever is appropriate in those circumstances to get our jail empty. We don't want anyone else here at the time of an emergency. So there aren't that many people left to deal with after the storm.

Then during the storm, we just wait for it to pass. Once it passes, we go out and check for anyone who may need help or assistance. Our main responsibilities are to take calls from people who are stranded in their homes, for trees blocking roadways, and for downed power lines. Then we work with the power company and whoever else to get the city back in line, up and running and operational again. Since everybody is out of town during the storm, we don't have to worry so much about looters breaking into people's homes and businesses and that kind of thing.

With most hurricanes, we are concerned with high tide and storm surge water coming in. Things along those lines.

Everybody talks about drainage systems. We were able to pass a bond issue after Harvey for improvements to prevent this type of devastation from occurring again. We spent $15,000,000 of that to improve our streets and drainage, but if there is another storm that drops 50 to 55 inches of rain in such a short period of time, we will most likely have flooding again. It is one of those things we are going to have to deal with. No one in the weather system -- state or county -- had any idea that this storm was going to go the way it did. This one caught us off guard.

Obviously, when we have a major incident happen, we typically have some fires. So we often assist the Fire Department. Once the storm passes, we work with the Street Department to get the streets cleared and get the roadways open. It is our aim to get this done as quickly as possible.

In this case, however, nobody had any warning. So there was no evacuation. We had one-third of the city underwater overnight with all of those people asking for help at the same time. When I arrived at the EOC that morning, there were already 500 calls for rescues that we needed to deal with. That's how it went, it was pretty much non-stop the entire time. It was a situation we had never dealt with before.

In this situation, search and rescue was our first priority. We dealt with finding families and getting people out of their flooded homes and vehicles. Then we needed places for these people to stay until the water receded and they were able to start picking up their lives again.

We don't normally do shelters because we send everybody out of town before the storm. With Harvey, we had to start managing shelters. We had to get them in place, get them up and running, including security, and we had no preparation time. We used many different avenues to accomplish this.

The rain started on that Saturday night. I was home with my wife, doing our normal business as were so many others. If I remember correctly, there was a fight on TV that night on Pay-per-view, so many people had gone to places to watch this fight. When they came out after the fight, the flooding had already started.

I remember that, about midnight, the Chief at the time, who was also a friend, called to say that he was headed to the office because there were power issues. He told me to be ready to come in at 6:00 am in the morning. So I pretty much treated it like any other night.

The next morning when I got up and saw the level of water, I knew this was not going to be normal. We had never had water that high on our street in South Shore since I had been here, and certainly nothing that rose that quickly. The water was almost up to my doorstop.

I went ahead and tried to drive my truck to the office. Every way I tried was blocked by high water. The water was so high it was impossible to know how to navigate. I ended up having to return home and call for a bigger truck to bring me in. The office arranged for a dump truck to come and get me, along with another one of our captains. That started a 21-hour shift before I went to sleep again. I was then able to sleep in my office for three hours before I got up and got busy again. The situation was a mess.

Fortunately, the water stopped just shy of the threshold of the door to our home. My wife was there and able to keep an eye on it and she was fine. We were fortunate not to have any damage or property loss.

Officer Corina Martinez kayaks down FM 518, with I-45 in the background, to get to work and begin aiding flood victims.
Photo courtesy of League City Police Department

There are many stories that happened out there in the water, but for me and the command staff, we were here managing things from inside this building. One of our officers, Corina Martinez, couldn't drive to work, so she got in a kayak and paddled herself in. When she got here, she immediately got to work, even though her house was flooded. Other officers came in and worked the storm even though their homes were flooded, too. Then, after the water started receding, they had to deal with their flooded homes just like everybody else.

The city has two or three high-water vehicles that are simply SUVs with lift kits. We have a SWAT vehicle, that they call an MRAP in the military. This one has been modified for civilian use. It is huge, so we used that as well.

The MRAP was a very valuable tool in rescue efforts. MRAP stands for "mine-resistant ambush protected" vehicle.
Photo courtesy of League City Police Department

We assisted other departments in making things happen that needed to happen. We ended up commandeering a couple of boats and anything else we could use to get to people.

We worried that this was going to be something like Hurricane Katrina, where we were going to have to go house to house after the storm, checking for bodies and things of that nature. Thank God, that is not what happened. Unfortunately, however, we did have a few deaths during the storm. One case may have been related to the flood waters, but we also had a suicide and a heart attack.

With Harvey, the National Guard came in with a platoon. I'm not sure how many soldiers they had, but they needed a place to house those soldiers. Since we had already emptied our jail, we had a place to house the National Guard. They had no complaints or issues whatsoever. This worked out well because when some of their special vehicles broke down, they were right here in our special vehicle bay to work on them. We had cots everywhere. Whatever they needed.

Then I remember that we had that group from Louisiana, the Cajun Navy, show up with their boats to help people. We had all kinds of people helping. We saw neighbors helping neighbors. Everyone was doing what they could to help folks and get people out.

Another thing I remember concerned the drainage system, because the system in this town was not nearly as good back then as what we have today. In anticipation of a hurricane, we always set up a command station on the west side of town at a school or something because of flooding. We knew that the area around the freeway floods quite easily. And if it did, we would be cut off from the west side of town. So by setting up on the west side of town, we would have a captain and his own team already in place, able to respond in case the roads were flooded. We then would have the same kind of deal set up on the east side of town so they could respond to all the east side calls, and the central part of town would be covered by the main station.

But in Harvey, we had everybody here. That deployment was not possible. So we did not have a response plan set out. We had people who didn't have their directions or know where to go. We had people going out all over the place. When I got here at 6:00 am, we had 500 calls waiting for a rescue.

When the Fire Department came in, they were trying to work with us. The Fire Department guys are used to doing rescue stuff. Those guys were getting out to make those calls. However, they didn't have computer access to our system. So when they went out to make those calls in their boats, for example, there was no way to clear the calls out of our system. The firemen had no way of contacting our Dispatch to say they had handled a particular call. So we had all these calls that were backing up and we didn't know which had been resolved. I had to send three or four officers downstairs to do nothing but call people back and ask if they still needed assistance or if someone had come to their aid. Ask them what their status was. That kind of thing. It was a mess from the get-go.

Mike was the Chief then and I was Assistant Chief, and we both had so much activity going on at the EOC that we were both working at the same time, which we did not normally do. We were both doing interior assignments to keep things rolling. We realized after we were both ready to crash and burn that we needed to set up a different system. So we agreed that, in the future when we have a situation like this, he would take 12 hours, then I would take 12 hours, or we can rotate or alternate from there, so we aren't both down at the same time. Typically now, we do 12 on and 12 off for about three days after a hurricane passes. Plus, we have the 12 hours before it hits.

We also try to let our people go back to their homes as quickly as we can. At some point during a hurricane, we try to make time for each officer to go check on his or her home and then get back to work, but that is for a normal type of hurricane. In Hurricane Ike for instance, I worked 12 hours and then stood in line for two hours to get gas for the generator. That would last for eight hours, and then I would do it all again the next day. So these are the things we get used to dealing with in a hurricane activation.

Any time we have a major incident like this happen, we do what we call a "hot wash" or debriefing at the end. We get everyone together and discuss all the hot issues that came up.

What were the issues that were handled well and where could we improve next time? We do this after every hurricane or SWAT issue. This helps us improve our future response.

This was the first hurricane we had experienced out of this building. It doesn't seem like a big deal, but this is the first city building built to withstand a category-four hurricane. All the other buildings we worked out of were not. When we were riding out a storm in those other buildings, you could hear the walls creaking. It was a wonder the walls didn't come down.

In the aftermath of an event, when things calm down, we try to do a damage assessment. We work hand in hand with all the other departments to determine how badly the city was hit.

We also have to consider that most businesses are closed after a major storm. Access to the things people need is shut. With Harvey, we had to figure out how to feed hundreds of people three meals a day for three to five days, or as long as it would take to get them through the shutdown. This is part of the logistics we had to deal with on top of everything else. It was a mess.

Typically, the EMC contracts with companies on the outside to come in and do what we or our businesses aren't able to do at the time. That was a great plan, but it was not always successful because a company would say we can't do that, or we can't make it in. In our evacuation plan, we would drive people out of town in school buses and the school system would help out with that.

After Harvey, we had the buses to evacuate people but no drivers. Boats were picking people up out of their houses and dropping them off. We had to have volunteers to drive buses to get people out of the spots where the boats dropped them off. Even the best of plans doesn't always work.

So we realized that we needed to start feeding people. I've been here a long time, so I started calling people I knew. I called the owner of Esteban's and said, "Hey Steve, we need some help. We need to feed a lot of folks here. Are you able to help out with that?"

Esteban's opened for us and allowed our folks to come in and eat. We made calls to other people that we knew and different folks were available. Those people really showed up. We had business owners who opened their businesses, and restaurant owners who fed hundreds of people. Everyone who could help, did. That's the thing that comes out of those types of tragedies and disasters. Anybody that could help, did. For months afterward, we gave recognition to businesses for the assistance they gave us during Hurricane Harvey.

One of the big problems with this storm was that everyone was impacted. Houston was flooded, too. It was strange the way this storm came in because Galveston wasn't impacted but everyone north of Galveston took it pretty hard. I don't know about Texas City, but La Marque, Dickinson and League City got hit really hard, and everywhere on into Houston. So it's not like the surrounding communities had teams of people they could send to help us out. We were all doing what we could to keep our heads above water, so to speak. No pun intended.

Some citizens had boats and stuff that they were able to use to rescue people. As I said, the Cajun Navy came in and just started helping folks. So many rescues did not go through us. There were people just going out and helping other folks any way they could. There is no telling how many folks came in from other places to assist.

I remember one thing that happened to one of our lieutenants.

I wasn't there but I enjoy telling this story. He was out in a boat with another guy. They thought they were in three, maybe four, feet of water. We had these little blow-up life vests that have sensors on them that will automatically trigger them to blow up if they need to. Our safety protocols require the officer to use the best of what is available.

Sean is a big guy, and he had a vest on over everything else. The other guy was in the driver's seat of the boat and obviously able to see the depth finder. Sean asked if they were "good." The other guy said, "Yes." So Sean jumps off the boat, thinking it was about four feet of water, but it was probably ten feet. When Sean went under, the life vest automatically filled with air choking him out. It wasn't around his chest: it was around that big ole head, choking him. The guy in the boat could see Sean wasn't in any real danger, but he couldn't do anything to help because he was laughing so hard.

There were so many different calls, and everybody was doing what they could just trying to help folks.

As I look back on this time, I remember additional bits and pieces of things we had to deal with. For instance, there is a pump station out in Bay Colony, and it was flooded. The concern was that things could get even worse if the power went out. If those pumps shut off, then the sewer would back up. Our guys were out in Bay Colony just working the pump stations because it was bad in Bay Colony, especially toward Dickinson. It was a mess. We had so many different things working at one time, it was unbelievable.

Throughout my years in the Department, I have taken part in tabletop exercises that help to get you mentally prepared to handle unexpected scenarios. I also went to a class at the Fire

Academy in Maryland, which was a FEMA training on hurricane response. Typically in the training, they will throw everything at you that they can. You got this happening here: You got that going on over there. And you have to figure out how you are going to deploy your people all at one time.

That was what responding to Hurricane Harvey was like. They always say they make these table-top exercises the worst possible scenarios – that it will never happen like that in real life. But that is exactly what Harvey was. Everything you can imagine was an issue all at the same time. We had so many complicating factors to deal with in this storm. It was a mess.

Officer Matt Kifer participated in many rescues, including pets that struggled in the deep water.
Here he hands a dog into the MRAP.
Photo courtesy of League City Police Department

Probably one-third of the people working this event had lost their homes or a good portion of their property to the flooding. As natural disasters come and go -- and they will continue to come and go -- we see how everybody comes together to help each other through it. This disaster was worse than some, but in this kind of hard times, we see how everyone tries to help others make it through the process.

Some handled it better than others. As we continue to move through life, each one of these disasters becomes another historical event we can learn from. That is also the time when true leaders rise to the top. You get to see what humans are really made of. Their personal opinions about people no longer matter: They are just there to help in any way they can. The individual that may not normally stop to help a stranger is doing everything he or she can.

I think when it is all said and done, for me, Hurricane Harvey was a bad one. I did not like this one. We were pinned against the wall the entire time we worked through it. There was no letting up.

Another thing I personally had to deal with happened when they sent the dump truck to get me that first morning. We also stopped to pick up one of our captains. I was trying to move around him in the truck and blew my ankle out. I had twisted it pretty bad. So with everything else going on, I had to find time to get to an Emergency Center to make sure I didn't damage it any further.

That's how it went with Harvey. You name it: If it could go wrong, it did. However, we learned a lot. We will be better prepared to respond to the next one.

As I said, I've been here my whole life. I went through the flood of '79. I was in Dickinson then and it was bad. Then in '83, it was also bad. That time, there were several feet of water in the streets. I don't know how many of these events this generation will go through, but as we move forward, the guys who previously led the way will start retiring. Then you get a new bunch of people who have not experienced those things. Hopefully, there are enough experienced people still left when the next event happens to walk everyone through what we have learned.

Still, every event is different. There are different nuances that come with every disaster. Sometimes it is a windstorm. Sometimes it is the rain. Sometimes you are going to have water pushed in by a hurricane. There are so many issues you deal with, and you won't know what they are until you are in the middle of them.

When we went through Hurricane Ike, one of our substations was the old Amegy Bank. We sent one third of our force over there. We did not consider what the roof of that building was made of. We just knew that it was a good structure for our guys to ride out the storm. However, the roof was an old asphalt-and-rock roof. When the wind started blowing, those rocks went everywhere. The rocks took out every window of every patrol car we had out there. These are the kind of things you cannot plan for but must deal with in short order.

We have a contingency plan for a category-five hurricane, and that includes taking about one-third of our force inland, somewhere like Huntsville, to weather out the storm. We have contingency plans for pretty much everything. But Harvey was different. It came in differently than any of the others. It came in "like a thief in the night" and it was not welcome.

III
Emergency Management During Harvey
by Ryan Edghill,
Emergency Management Coordinator

I have been with the City since 2013. Emergency Management is a support function, and my job is to coordinate information and resources. The Emergency Operations Center (EOC) is housed at 555 West Walker in the Public Safety Building.

My initial observations during the onset of Hurricane Harvey showed that things were starting to look more and more serious as we held three to four daily briefings.

Harvey had broken across the Yucatan and was looking, at first, like a South Texas storm. Lots of people didn't know how bad it was going to be, but we in the EOC thought we knew how bad it would be. As the storm got closer and closer, the rainfall projections got higher and higher, and about two days before landfall, we knew the prediction was for about 12 inches of rain over four days. We thought we could handle it.

My job was to translate everything into field tactics and make sure everyone had the stuff they needed. I also had to get to the Mayor and make sure he got the whole picture of whatever was going on at the time. The job is stressful, and the hours are long.

At one point, I came into my office and tried to get a couple hours of sleep. I couldn't perform all of the required functions because things were happening so quickly. It was overwhelming.

There were no resources. We couldn't get the tools we needed. We were cut off. Once Clear Creek flooded, no one could get here. The phones never stopped ringing. We couldn't keep up with the phone calls. Then the tower that provides emergency service for the area ran out of fuel.

But we did have National Guard locally here and were able to house them in the jail. During the sheltering operations, at any given point we had well over 10,000 individuals in shelters.

Galveston Island was not heavily impacted like the rest of us north of there, so they set up C-130s to conduct air operations in Galveston and were able to fly people to Dallas to get them out of the area.

I spent the whole time in the EOC in City Hall, including 20- to 22-hour days, with a couple of hours trying to sleep.

We used all methods of communication at our disposal, including phones, TV, internet and National Weather Service. The EOC has eight cable feeds. We had daily phone calls with Galveston emergency managers and state resources.

Our catering contractors couldn't reach us to feed staff, so volunteers went around town trying to find places that were open to get food for our people. Local restaurants also donated food.

One of the biggest challenges was donations management, which can become its own disaster after the disaster. We used the old, closed Kroger as a donation center. We had an agreement before the storm with a group to manage donations, but it still wasn't adequate.

An incredible number of volunteers came from everywhere. Webster had less impact than we did, and many people from there helped out when they could. The Red Cross also supported us. Volunteers were mostly citizens who were not impacted. There were actually a lot more than we knew about, like the Cajun Navy.

Some volunteers dropped off the people they rescued at the

FM 646 overpass out in the rain. Another volunteer effort turned the front of the new HEB into a makeshift reception center to get these people into shelters. Volunteers and HEB staff helped.

City staff who rescued people were able to use available city shelters and Hometown Heroes, but other volunteers who were rescuing people didn't know where to take them and had to find shelters.

League City residents are happy to see
Officers Matt Maggiolino and Noe Perez
arrive in the MRAP to take them to safety.
Photo courtesy of League City Police Department

Shelter volunteers included a huge group of city residents as well as some city councilors. Their attitude was always "with volunteer spirit, with neighbors helping neighbors, we can get through anything."

Debris management operations were also huge, with 20% of homes taking in some type of water. We had 175,000 cubic yards of construction debris to deal with, as well as 96 million pounds of construction and demolition debris.

There were medication and health issues to manage in the shelters. Galveston County Health District now has a core staff of people who can go from shelter to shelter during a crisis to help people with medical needs.

Pets were also cared for. After Hurricane Katrina, it had become law that you cannot turn away a person you are rescuing who has a pet, but they must have a crate.

So finally, after five days, I went home to my family, north of the creek.

We've made a lot of improvements and solved a lot of problems since then. We have a dedicated logistics staff, whose sole responsibility is to get stuff in an emergency. There wasn't a good plan in place for Harvey, and what we had didn't fit the extreme nature of Harvey. We were fortunate that volunteers stepped up and solved the problems. It was an incredible effort of creative thinking.

We've added six new rain gauges in the area, so next time we will know where the worst areas are and can pull the trigger faster to get things. We've also made some agreements to take staff and city vehicles outside of the area, so we don't lose equipment like we did.

IV
It was A Flood to Me
by Ryan Smith,
Director, Information Technology/Facilities

I remember the first time I heard of Hurricane Harvey very well. It was the night that Harvey hit and -- I'm drawing a blank, I think it was a Saturday night -- I was on Main Street in a neighborhood in Highland Terrace. My friends and I were there for the fantasy football and fight night.

I started seeing alerts on my phone about the weather. So I decided, "I gotta go outside and see what's going on."

I started listening to the radio traffic and thought, "I gotta go home."

As I went outside, it occurred to me, "The water's up to my running boards. I gotta go to work!"

I pulled out onto Main Street and as I drove, where the road dips down, water splashed on my hood. I pulled into the middle lane and, when I turned onto the main street, the Police Department called and said, "We don't have any power."

Then it hit me, and I responded, "You must be on generator power. I'll be there in a few minutes."

I pulled onto Walker and the road was flooded, so I turned into the City Hall back parking lot, parked and grabbed a city car and went across the street. I could hear the generator in City Hall running, but the whole building was dark. I was in flip flops and shorts and tried using my phone as a flashlight until I could get a real flashlight and decided, "Hey, let me see if the utility power is functional."

Officers Pat Self, Noe Perez and Matt Maggiolino
wade through knee-deep water.
Photo courtesy of League City Police Department

I was able to switch them back to utility power and get them working. I then saw Ryan Edghill from the EOC (Emergency Operations Center) and he said, "Thankfully you're here. It's just me right now."

I said, "Well, I solved the generator problem for now."

And that's how I found out about Harvey.

To me, Harvey was not a hurricane. It was a flood. And I certainly wasn't expecting that kind of flooding in League City -- ever.

So the first thing I did was to regroup with Ryan because I'm on the EOC team and my first question was, "What do we do, because the wheels are off the bus right now?"

Dispatch physically backs up to the EOC in the office, and I could hear that Dispatch was overwhelmed. I immediately knew to start calling some of my people in the Facilities team and IT. None of them could get to the office at that time other than, I think, Scott Crawford, and I don't remember if anybody else made it in.

I then called City Manager John Baumgartner. He didn't answer his phone, so I called his wife. She answered and I said, "Wake him up now. It's horrible. He needs to get here."

He could barely get there.

We were all up and working for the next 30 hours straight, and it was just a blur for those 30 hours.

The EOC also decided to open Hometown Heroes as a shelter area for displaced people, so I sent Scott Crawford over there. He reported back that the gates were closed, and he couldn't get in. He decided to go back down Route 96 and try another gate.

I don't remember the timeline, but someone soon called me and said, "We can't find Scott."

My quick response was, "I'm going to head that way."

So I headed down FM 96 and unlocked the gate. As I did, I turned and saw Scott's Ford F150, submerged in water midway up the driver's window.

Now, Scott's a big boy and I'm like -- I still get chills right now thinking about that moment -- I whispered, "Please don't let him be in this vehicle."

I turned and looked around and I saw someone in a yellow slicker suit walking in the median. I turned the truck around and he got in. And he was crying, "I'm going to be fired."

"No, you're not. You're alive. Get in and dry off."

He said, "I don't have a phone or anything because everything got lost or soaked in the car."

I responded, "It's okay, we'll figure it out. Can you take over Hometown Heroes until we figure things out? We are about to start dropping people off there."

I then turned to coordinating with the people in the Fire Marshall's Office to put things together and assist everybody who was calling.

I can remember at one point we needed some airboats. I called my cousin (and woke him up) saying, "Hey, we need airboats for rescues and my airboat doesn't work. Can you help?"

He quickly responded, "We've got mechanics here. Hook it up and get it to the mechanic shop."

"You're serious?" I asked.

"It's that bad. I agree, we are gonna need it," he confirmed. He took it to John Oregon, they got it running, and we were able to get it out to do rescues.

At some point we tried to get to Fire Station #5. The power was shut off and we had to get the people out of there. But it was flooded, and we couldn't get there.

We also needed food because our staff was hungry, so we called the manager of the Super Kroger on FM 96 to see if he could come in. The manager said, "Ryan, we are on an island here in Westover Park and Westwood."

I said, "We're going to go to Fire Station #4. I'll send the National Guard to get you and then we'll all meet up at the store."

The National Guard had already been here for a while. They were sleeping in our jail (I know because I have pictures of them somewhere, including all the military vehicles parked around the Police Department.)

We were able to get the manager to Kroger and, as we got near, there were people standing out front. We told them, "Hey, we're coming in a side door. We've got to feed our people first. Then we will be with you."

They were all understanding because they knew how hard we were working to help them.

Andrew Hernandez and I loaded up the food, but there was only one way to go to the west side of town. You couldn't go down League City Parkway and Walker was underwater, so we had to take FM 518 to Calder, go under the overpass and get to it that way because FM 518 and I-45 was underwater, and as soon as you came over the overpass at FM 646 and the freeway, that was under water, too.

So many of the community businesses helped us out where they could. Plenty of people did. Esteban's was phenomenal. It seemed like they fed us almost around the clock. We would just show up there and eat and go. They're one of the best.

At one point, something went wrong with the AC in the jail. The humidity and the fire alarm had triggered something and shut it off. In the middle of the night, I was on the phone with our fire alarm contractor, trying to unwire the fire alarm so that the AC could come on for the military.

But we were able to keep the main city buildings operating so the City staff had power. At one point, I remember I noticed that it was flooding worse and went to check on our cars. They were up on the curb/sidewalk against the back wall of City Hall because the whole parking lot was under water. I noticed that one car, a four-door Mercedes, had water coming up to it. The car belonged to Paul Menzis, our Planning Director. So I went running through the building, looking for him. All the lights were off, and I don't know if the building had power at that time or not. But I found Paul Menzis, asleep in a room.

"Paul! Get up, move your car. It's flooding," I yelled.

I'm thinking that the high water continued for around 50

hours or somewhere in that timeline, because John and I were up probably 32 hours before we finally got a break. We went home to just shower and get rid of the PTSD for a few minutes and check on things there. Just to get away from it. It was horrible.

John and I didn't participate in any rescues or interact with the public, like in front of Kroger or other places. So once the water finally started going down, John and I began to drive around and assess the city.

We started assessing city buildings, taking pictures and cataloging, with comments like, "This building is closed. We will have to find a new building for Public Works, and a new building for Fire Station #5 for now."

We began working with HR and Insurance to figure out, "Hey, what are we going to do?"

I know one of the best things that came up, though. I think it was Monday or Tuesday. I talked with Kroger. They had closed their building at I-45 and FM 518 and opened a new location. They gave us the full lease of their old building, or they were still on the lease, and they subleased it to us for a dollar to use.

So we went into recovery mode and arranged to get food dropped off. We got a forklift and a pallet jack delivered so we could start using that whole facility as a distribution center for food and water and clothing, all that stuff.

I can remember another thing. There's a waiter I knew, he still works at Mr. Sombrero's and I had pictures with him when he and his wife came into the center. They had a newborn and they had lost everything. We got them a crib and a mattress, some clothing and baby formula. We still talk about that family to this day.

What I really remember from that time is how we all united to come together as a team. It didn't matter what your job scope was, you would see our City Manager cutting up boxes and throwing them in a dumpster. You would see us doing whatever we needed to do to help people in need. We didn't care about a title; we came together however we needed to make it work. And not just the city, but this whole county and then other states. So many people came together to help other people out.

There were 18-wheelers from several states that were full of supplies. We all helped with unloading at the Kroger location, then volunteers showed up to help people get whatever they needed. Others helped by picking people up, giving them a ride, whatever they needed.

Others helped people with their damaged houses. I think maybe 8,000 homes in the city were damaged. But you'd have to check with Development for a better number. My family and I were blessed, we were not personally affected.

In the end, I think the communication and how we worked together was a very positive thing. It was just a strange event. It was not your typical hurricane. I've worked several of those and I don't think you could plan or predict this. But we just kept kicking the ball down the road and we didn't stop. We adapted. We overcame, no matter what.

The Public Works team is phenomenal. Jody Hooks' team. Their building was flooded, so we shuffled them to the Kroger and then to another building. They were out there the whole time, partnering and working together, with Fire and EMS in the middle of it.

There was one story I remember about a Public Works guy, I think it was Rideaux Princeton, who was in a dump truck. There's a photo of it somewhere where the water's up to the driver's window of the dump truck. These guys are not used to doing rescues and he's scared. Another story is about a fire truck where water's halfway up the truck. It's flooded in the middle of FM 517, and people just kept on going.

And other stories, such as a friend of mine who lives in Bay Ridge. He went to bed and when he woke up and put his feet down, he had two feet of water in his house.

Looking back on it, I think we shouldn't take any storm for granted. Some people in the area were new and they might not have experienced a storm like this, so it's always better to be over-prepared. But it wasn't just us; it was several cities that I've talked to, like Webster and Pasadena, that took it for granted.

It's kind of crazy. For instance, on Friday it was windy and a little bit rainy and some things were shutting down. Then Saturday it was all nice. People were saying, "We're going to open up. We're going to go out. It's fight night." So we went out.

Then afterwards, you drive through Bay Colony and see all the ruts in the grass, tire marks running between trees or a car in the middle of a retention pond where, more than likely, those guys were racing to get home. More than likely, their wives called them saying their house was flooded or the road was flooded. I remember this black Escalade just in the middle of a retention pond once it had drained. The guy hadn't known where he was going, and he just fell off into the pond.

In the end, our community was resilient. It came back stronger than ever. We passed a big bond issue to improve drainage and I don't think you'll ever see a storm like this again, that's my opinion.

To me, it was not a hurricane – it was a flood. It wasn't even hardly any wind, but it was still one to go down in the history books, for sure.

V

Be Prepared and Have Your Emergency Kit
by Jody Hooks, Director, Public Works

I first heard about a thing called Hurricane Harvey probably a week or so before it made landfall, because in Public Works, we are weather watchers. Weather is everything to us and impacts us immensely, both in our utility operations as well as the drainage aspect.

Like right now, we are looking at a system that might come into the Gulf, and we're already thinking about it and watching it. It was the same thing with Harvey. Probably up to a week prior to landfall, we were watching it dance around.

We thought we were fine, because it was hitting further south, near Corpus. Then it made landfall, and kind of meandered this way, along the entire Texas coast. But you could say that's when we first started talking about it.

So whenever that happens, we automatically start thinking about the precautions we're going to take. We've been through many storms, going back as far as Hurricane Rita in 2005 and Hurricane Ike in 2008. So Public Works is pretty in tune with preparations.

We start with the basics, like fueling up all our emergency standby generators for our wastewater facilities, our water facilities, and any other facility that serves us. And then, the wastewater treatment plants, lift stations and water plants.

We start looking at all the things on the ground that might blow around or create damage or hurt somebody. We tidy that up.

We start thinking about all our construction projects that are going on, because we need to prepare them, as well. And we usually coordinate with our project management group here to make sure our contractors are getting everything in order.

Then we start thinking about food and shelter, wherever we're going to ride it out. Obviously, Public Works is really five major disciplines, and we're at multiple locations. So we make sure that everybody has food, water and fuel for their vehicles.

Then we make sure we have our primary "ride-out" teams identified. These are the groups that stay during the storm, so we can respond as soon as the storm breaks. We have a secondary group that's allowed to get their families out of harm's way and then they prepare to come back as soon as possible.

Streets were flooded throughout the geographic area.
This street is in Santa Fe.
Photo courtesy of C. Chapman

So the day the storm hit…. Let me think back. We knew the rain was coming, and probably experienced it the day before a little bit. But the night that we really had the heaviest impact of rain, we were gearing up and already getting reports from my utilities about what was going on at the plants.

We began to get street flooding early on. This triggers us to start getting our people and our high-water vehicles ready. And before the sun even came up that morning, we were already losing vehicles to flooding, because a lot of the major highways were covered in water.

The second thing that happened – and this was a first for us -- our Police Department had a lot of their patrol officers' vehicles flood at their houses. Because Harvey was -- whatever they want to call it -- a "once-in-a-thousand-year storm," people were not prepared.

Officer Jason Kifer, equipped in waders and communications equipment, walks flooded streets looking for people in need.
Photo courtesy of League City Police Department

They had parked some of their patrol cars on the curbside in front of their houses and on the low part of their drives. By the time morning came, there was a high percentage of patrol officers who were stranded because their cars were flooded. And this was during some of the heaviest rains.

Public Works was tasked to get some of our large dump trucks or anything we had that could handle high water. We were then sent out to retrieve police officers and bring them in. So that was the first impact to Public Works: first-responder, hero-type deals.

We began by picking up police officers, and that transformed into picking up people. At this time of the morning, water was getting near to houses. By the second round of us going out later in the morning, water was already in some houses.

It seemed that, in any neighborhood we went into, there were people very panicked about coming out of their neighborhood. So we helped people at least get to high ground in their neighborhoods. It was a pretty unique experience.

We're not really in the rescue service. But I guess human nature and the public works aspect of it just kind of takes over. We have a lot of great people in our group, and they were superheroes that day, right along with the Police Department, Fire Department and the EMS.

So we helped with the rescues. As the morning progressed, we experienced flooding and the things associated with the storm like lightning and thunder, electrical loss, etc. My utility groups were constantly out there checking things, making sure the lift stations were running. (Everybody wants a lift station running because that keeps our sanitary sewer system operating.)

Because it's all about the wastewater. The guys at the wastewater plant were making sure the plant kept running. The guys in the water distribution system were making sure we didn't lose power, so we didn't lose water system pressure.

That's our battle. To keep the utilities going. So they were all out there during the hurricane. And a big concern, of course, was making sure that our guys were as safe as they could be. But once we started losing vehicles, obviously we had to stop, think and plan cautiously on the things we could safely get to.

(Luckily, the city now has very upgraded, up-to-date infrastructure, where we can monitor things remotely, using SCADA systems that allow us to see what's going on at most of our sites without having to be there in person. SCADA means System, Data and Acquisition System. It's a monitoring system for remote sites.)

By around noon, we even had people starting to show up at some of our facilities. Their whole neighborhoods were flooded, and they were panicked.

By that time, the City teams had begun coordinating different drop-off sites, because that first day was just havoc. I mean, the EOC was up and running, working to figure out where to put all these displaced people. Now we were kind of tasked to transport some of those people.

At the time, we were located at 1535 Dickinson Avenue. Although our building didn't flood, the road to and from the building was covered in water. So it was really just emergency vehicles traversing that road. Then it was mostly us: As they were bringing people to our building, we were hauling them to other locations.

To begin with, we put people in any open spot we could find. The people in our EOC were amazing. They started working with the school district, Hometown Heroes, any large-volume space we had. They found places and started organizing and dropping people off. The coordination effort at the time was critical, and the results were amazing.

As a leader, I was just constantly looking at all my different areas, just kind of absorbing what they were experiencing, and trying to make sure everybody was safe. I also wanted to try to help talk people through things that they had never seen before.

A very important part of our work during the storm centered around the call center we set up so members of the public could call the city. We set it up through Ryan Smith of IT/Facilities. In my memory, Jeanne Griffin stayed up 30 hours straight working the call center.

We had different people working shifts on it. It was almost like a 311, but sometimes we would have calls come in that were for South Houston or other areas that we did not even handle. We had to try to switch them over to another department. Or during the biggest part of the storm, we had to have people tell them that nobody was going out and we couldn't do anything right then. But once the storm calmed a little, we would relay the information to the Police Department where people needed help. So we helped filter some of the calls for them.

IT set that up and Public Works manned it. Jeanne and some of our other ladies manned the call center during that time. That was pretty crazy in itself.

Jeanne was mostly on Dickinson Avenue, just seeing people come in, wet and scared. People came in with their animals, too. We had one lady in a wheelchair come in, because they couldn't get to Hometown Heroes or any of the other places. The drivers had to drop them off with us. But all in all, people had good spirits.

What stands out about the storm in my memory? That our people were actually able to make it into work. I've been here a long time, I started in the Utilities Group. So riding out storms? I've worked every storm that came through here for 30-plus years. Those were not a big deal. But the magnitude of what was going on with this storm was certainly different. And what stands out for me? That people were actually able to make it into work.

Another memory. Some of our dump truck drivers drove around areas of this city with water up to the bottom of the doors. In a dump truck! We had a couple of guys stall and they had to get out and be rescued themselves. Everybody thinks, "Oh, it's just water, I'm just going to jump out." But this time, people were a little bit terrified. The water had some current to it, so there were things nobody had really experienced before.

I tried to adapt our procedures to the safety aspect of the situation and started telling people, "Look, we're not trained rescue people. You really got to think of where you're going, and work along with Fire and PD. They are trained rescue people."

And yet, human nature still took over. I mean, our guys would be working their way into a flooded neighborhood to get to a lift station. From the big highway to there, they would still help people, no matter what. And they did a great job.

I didn't participate in any of the rescues, I wasn't on the dump trucks. I spent most of my time in the EOC but did go out riding and evaluating with Bo Bass, the Assistant City Manager, sometimes.

When we did go out evaluating, we carried and distributed food, constantly working with the EOC, and just managing all the activities within my group, staying in touch with them. Did I carry anybody out of a house? No, I didn't.

I have worked all these storms, but the biggest impact is what you see in our people. Not only were they away from their families, but their loved ones were at home in flooded houses. And they were upset, terrified and devastated. Our people normally work storms when their families are safe. But this was different. Some of them had a hard time focusing on what they were doing because they had turmoil in their household or with their family members.

There's a lot of good people in Public Works, a lot of strong people, and we accommodated what we could. If people had to get home to their family, we didn't stop them. We told them, "You need to do what's right for yourself. Stay safe, take care of your family and house. Then try to get back to us." And most people did that.

I think we have 138 people total in Public Works. And I think we had, if I remember the number right, as many as 80-plus of those working, while the others were dealing with their homes -- or trying to. And they tried to get back and help us when they could.

I can't think of how many people in Public Works either lost their houses or had direct family members that were equally devastated. Some people who didn't even have an impact themselves spent the next few months helping others who did. The impact and recovery was just spread out for a long time.

Personally, I was very blessed. My house didn't flood and we were fine. My extended family was also safe; their houses did not flood.

It was hard work, too. That's always the case with storms. It could be utilities or draining streets or traffic. We worked till the dangers were done for, or as much as possible. We worked to keep the streets safe, and our water system safe, and our wastewater collection treatment system safe.

We were managing hours, tracking how many hours people were working. And some of our people, you had to really make them go home with, "You got to. You have to take a break," because they would keep going and going and going. Or "Hey, go home. Serve your family. Then get back to us."

That was another unique thing Public Works did. We delivered, I want to say, thousands of pizzas -- and food that restaurants said, "Hey, come get this. Where do you need it?"

People were cooking for us. Restaurants that had no customers but had power were cooking all the food they could to give away, rather than have it go bad or just sit there during a time of need.

We took food to distribution points for our first responders and our city. It wasn't only Public Works, and it wasn't only first responders. Everybody in the city was working. It was just a full citywide effort.

Again, Ryan Edghill and the EOC worked with other emergency connections for food. Sometimes, as we got further into recovery and word got out about how the Texas coast was devastated, not only did food come from locals, but it was coming from nationwide, and I'm sure you've heard the stories. In fact, we actually created collection and distribution centers for all those 18-wheelers that were coming in with tons of supplies. It was just an immense outpouring of help, from all over the country. It was amazing.

In terms of logistics, this was actually a unique storm because, although a lot of people lost their houses, a lot of people didn't. And the level of compassion in this city was amazing. The people who still had dry homes and electricity and could see others suffering, they stepped up. It really showed that this is a great community. I've never seen such compassion. It is a great story.

One of the biggest issues we dealt with actually didn't begin until after the flood waters had receded. And that was debris management. If you think about the approximately 8,000 homes that were flooded, damaged or lost, and all the damaged furniture, etc., that is just mass quantities of things that are ruined. All the construction, building and household materials had to be brought to the curb for disposal.

Trash piles consisted of once-loved items as well as construction debris, and told a heartbreaking story of each home's damage.
Photo courtesy of Gary Macdonell

The magnitude of that was probably one of the largest things I've experienced in years, from a Public Works aspect. We had a contractor to manage that, but Public Works had to address a certain percentage of that, too. And that went on for weeks in some areas, months in others. Harvey happened, I think, on August 27 and 28, and I think we finished with the debris removal in December or in January 2018. At least four solid months.

So debris management was big. In addition, our own facilities were flooded and we lost some lift stations as well as water distribution facilities. It seemed like a never-ending process to get them back up and running, and then restored. So that went on for months, as well.

The drainage aspect went on for two to three years, with all of us working, all of our heavy equipment, all of our resources, and all of our streets and drainage crews. We worked on a lot of our storm sewer systems as well as a lot of our outfall ditch systems.

We had at least three years of just working maintenance issues and doing evaluations for big FEMA-related projects.

When I think back over the event and its aftermath, I think we also learned a lot. We learned what our measure of response should be. Since Harvey, we've had a couple of hurricanes that were not direct hits, but the level of preparation today is kind of automatic: It's the highest level.

For example, when Winter Storm Uri came, that was an equally unique, devastating type of storm, and all of the great things that we did and learned during Harvey resurfaced. It was like we were fine-tuned by Harvey, and we kind of built from that.

The other thing is, don't forget, that during the pandemic, when everything was shut down, Public Works was not shut down. We worked every day. We were in harm's way, like every other first responder. Even in that instance, we were kind of programmed from Harvey because we had learned a lot. Through these ensuing years, I've seen the progression of it.

Yes, we learned from previous storms like Ike and Katrina, but to me, Harvey was the baseline of our response and a measure of how prepared we now are. Now, through everything else -- winters, freezes, pandemics, different storms – we're ready. I'm not saying we are invincible, but we are ready. And it seems natural.

One additional thought. You know when they say, "Be prepared and have your emergency kit." Well, Jody Hooks always says to all his guys to "Be prepared, have enough food for three or four days, and be self-sufficient. But also -- have a life jacket." I think Harvey was the source of that advice.

One final thing I would like to say is that the American Public Works Association in the last few years has made a grand effort to try to promote the work of Public Works' first responders. In 2002, after 9/11, President Bush made a presidential declaration (HSPD-8) on behalf of first responders. It says, "Public Works are considered emergency first responders," and what did we do in Harvey? We were out there, in some cases even before the police.

We are not saying, "Hey, we want to be considered the police and fire." We're just saying that during these natural disasters, we're right out there with them. And at that given time, we are --and were -- first responders. So I bring this up just to bring to people's attention that Public Works people are out there helping people in need.

VI
Tenacity in Spite of the Challenges
by John Baumgartner, City Manager

The first time I heard about Hurricane Harvey was from the Weather Service advisories. We heard it was in the Caribbean and then in the Gulf. We asked out of curiosity, "What category storm is it?"

Then it hit down close to Rockport and just kind of stalled out, maybe on Thursday or Friday, giving them intense rain while we were getting a smattering of rain. And then I think we grew a little bit complacent because the winds weren't quite as strong as was expected. It backed up and stalled, so we thought, "Oh, we're okay."

But then it turned around and came up the coast. We watched it all day Friday and all day Saturday as it continued to rain, but the worst of it was to the south and west of us. And we thought, "Hey, it's just going to be a bunch of rain."

I finally got a phone call in the middle of the night, Saturday night, like 11:00 pm, saying, "Hey, this thing is just all over us."

My home was not personally affected by the flooding, so I've been blessed. I was lucky from that perspective, and it gave me opportunity to focus on the community, which is probably where I was needed at that time.

I live over in South Shore, so to get to the office, I came FM 2094 to 270 to 96 because all of those roadways sit pretty high off the ground. The ditches were full and the lightning was exploding as I went over the railroad bridge and I couldn't see anything. I was just trying to stay between the lines on the roadway.

I got to the EOC somewhere between 11:00 pm and midnight, and there were people and police officers in the lobby. There were people whose cars had stalled out and they were walking in and they were wet from the waist down. It was that much water that quickly. It was just crazy.

So the first day I got there around midnight, and I finally got a chance to get four or five hours of sleep at the EOC on Sunday night around midnight.

I stayed in the building and didn't go home because we were getting reports from all over. One call I remember, although I forget the guy's name, was from a couple of the Public Works heroes (I call them that) saying, "Hey, we're having to take care of the people that have been displaced from their homes and they're at 646 and I-45."

So we sent him over to open up Hometown Heroes as kind of an emergency shelter. In the course of doing that, he ended up going off the road on FM 96. The water was up to the window in his truck. He had to literally climb out the window headfirst and soaking wet. Ryan Smith found him going up the highway toward Hometown Heroes, still working to get the gates unlocked and make sure we had access to it.

There are lots of stories like that. There's another about a gentleman who was driving a dump truck and the dump truck got flooded out when he was two or three miles from Dickinson Avenue. He was on the west side of town. His name was Princeton, I think. His radio got wet. His phone got wet. And he had to walk back to the Public Works Service Center to report back to work, because he couldn't communicate with anybody.

So he leaves a flooded-out dump truck, gets into waist-deep water, walks back and goes right back to work. Those were the types of heroes that we saw through this whole storm. Those were both first-day stories, Saturday night or Sunday morning, I think.

One of the problems we dealt with was how to get people out of the houses that were flooding and the neighborhoods that were flooded. We didn't have enough high-water vehicles to deal with the amount of flooding that we had. So we converted dump trucks and Public Works trucks. We put ladders into the backs of the trucks and people climbed onto the ladders and sat in the backs of the trucks.

At one time, and I know I'm not going to get the numbers quite precise, I think we had 1200 calls waiting in Dispatch for help. People waiting with service requests. So we literally drove to the dispatchers' houses to get them and bring them to the office in our high-water vehicles.

One of the dispatchers, Dani's her first name, can tell the story about riding in the back of the dump truck to get to work with the rain just pouring down on top of her. I mean, that's how much commitment there was. And then there was another, I think it was a police officer, who actually walked from the Webster area across the railroad bridge to get to work.

We maybe got 15 inches of rain in a six-hour period and then it quit for a little bit, and then we got another eight inches.

"Disaster brings out the very best in people" is what I like to say. These are the kind of stories we heard during the initial part of the event. Neighbors helping neighbors and neighbors helping us, working together to deal with the initial onslaught of the whole storm. If we needed a boat, we went out and commandeered a boat, with a message to the owner that, "Hey, we'll catch up with you next week." And that was OK.

And then obviously, the Police Department stories and the

Fire Department rescue stories.

So both Sunday night and Monday night were just tremendous rain events. I think the water came up higher the second night than it did the first night. I was again at the EOC, and we were working to communicate with the public, the City Council and the staff. There was so much stuff coming in all at one time. It was incredible.

I'm actually new to the Gulf Coast. I've only been here ten years. What they tell me about hurricanes is that every storm is different, so get ready for the hurricane. We know it's coming; we see it's coming. We even know there's going to be a lot of rain with it.

The City does have a hurricane plan. We try to make sure that our fuel tanks are topped off, that we've done our preventative maintenance on those storm sewer outfalls and stuff like that, and that we have people in place.

We secure our buildings, secure our equipment so it doesn't flood. But the best-laid plans…. We had a number of vehicles that flooded, such as police cars that were at people's houses. That was the most common. So we try to secure the equipment beforehand. Then the stuff that floods during the storm are all "measured risk" things that occur when someone is driving through high water to get someplace.

The plan includes having a "ready reaction team" in place so when the winds get up north of 50 or 60 miles an hour, we quit being out there, because then we would be putting people at risk. We try to get people pre-positioned so when the storm subsides, they can go right to work and they've got the tools and equipment necessary to do that.

One of the interesting lessons learned had to do with the

extreme duration of the event. It started here Saturday night, Sunday morning, and it went on for about three days. Just trying to get the people that were here fed during that time was a challenge. The public was very generous, and they brought lots of food to the police stations and fire stations and to the Public Works folks. Because the people that drive the dump trucks and clean out the storm sewers and get the debris out of the road and stuff were working alongside the police and firefighters. Whether it was rescue activities or just trying to maintain passageways on the roadways. They were working the same long, long hours.

Public Works staff isn't as big as the police and firefighters so they just went until they couldn't go anymore. The logistics and keeping them fed were both challenges. One of those interesting things that we learned was that we probably didn't pre-position supplies and food as well as we should because during the storm, the grocery stores were closed. The restaurants were closed. There wasn't a ready, accessible source of food.

What we did have were MREs, Meals Read to Eat, that we get from FEMA to help sustain them in the worst of the weather.

So now we do a lot of logical planning things. Do we have fuel? Do we have food? Is our equipment secured? Are people secured?

Another part of the story took place inside the EOC itself. It was overrun with information coming in, whether it was people needing help, decisions to be made, how and when to assign assets. Sometimes, as I mentioned before, we needed to commandeer an asset, such as somebody's boat. We try to ask permission, but if there's nobody to ask, we need to make the command decision in order to help people.

Some of the questions that we dealt with: How to get

resources from the state and from FEMA? Stuff is breaking, how to get replacements? Can we open Hometown Heroes as an emergency shelter? We can't get across town because the city's been cut in half due to floodwaters, but we need something on the east side. Can we get in touch with the school district? If we can't get someone from the school district, can we break into the school? And who's responsible for making decisions that in the normal course of business you wouldn't do, but in the course of an emergency you would do?

So those are the type of issues and questions that came to me in the EOC. Again, because there were not enough resources and you had to make decisions on how resources were allocated. We had to figure out how to get people here. We had to decide how to communicate with the public, with FEMA, with the state, with our City Council members and other elected officials.

We were doing twice-daily "push" messages out on Facebook. There wasn't one single way to communicate with everybody. There's not one method that reaches everybody. So you do the very best you can with what you have at the time. As I said, the first two or three days were all just crisis management and reaction to the different things that came up.

We also talked about feeding people. And so somewhere in there, maybe Day Two, we got in touch with the owner of Esteban's and he said he had food but no customers. So he cooked tacos and stuff for all of the city workers. And they were able to go in there one at a time to get food. There wasn't a lot of menu choices, but that was OK. It was "Here's what you're getting." Those were the type of things that we were doing in the immediate crisis time.

Once the flood water began to go down, we were into the

whole recovery thing. The aftermath was really interesting. First there was an assessment phase, and that meant assessing the basic city facilities and making sure that we could get them up and running. The sewer plant had 12 inches of water, so we had to ask, "Were the electrical systems compromised? Would it run? Would it work?"

We had lift stations that had been completely flooded and asked the question, "Would they turn on and would they work?" And if they wouldn't, we had to ask, "Then what?" Because then we started dealing with different problems.

Again, back to opening the grocery stores. We had to ensure that they could be secured. At one time we had probably as many as 600 people at Hometown Heroes. That meant that I had 600 people who needed to be fed. The biggest questions: "How do I get them fed -- every day -- and how long are they going to stay?"

Once the storm subsided, the numbers at Hometown Heroes went down pretty quickly. There was also a Red Cross shelter at the Methodist Church on South Shore Boulevard and FM 518. We were responsible for providing security for those facilities. One of the people there was a lady who had brought some type of large bird with her, I'll call it a parrot. I even went and got bird food for her.

The whole situation with the grocery stores was a challenge. They eventually let people in, but there were long lines. I have to say that the grocery stores worked really well with the city. They sold us groceries to supply the folks that were working here and to supply the shelter folks. So again, a real community effort. And again, like I said, the Kroger folks were tremendously generous, H-E-B folks were generous, too.

And then the next piece of that is the question, "What are we doing in the community to assist everyone with the recovery and getting things moving again?" Immediately after the storm, we did assessments. For example, we worked with the school district on their issues, assessed what was flooded and how to get their buildings opened again.

The big piece for us with recovery was debris removal as well as getting our contracts with CrowderGulf set up and enacted so we would get reimbursed from FEMA. Someone probably has more precise numbers, but I'm thinking nearly $5 million worth of debris removal. We needed the big trucks and the big trailers with drivers and people to monitor the work. Then we had to pay them and get our reimbursements.

"Mucking out" began as soon as people could get back into their homes, saving what they could, and putting the rest in big piles by the road for pick-up.
Photo courtesy of Bruce Moran

So we got to work with City Council. We put some money into a Harvey fund and then we used those dollars to pay the folks. And then we had to follow up to make sure that the community got reimbursed.

Debris removal probably lasted through December. One issue we dealt with occurred when a whole house was flooded. The owners pushed as much debris out to the street as they could. The debris people did a pretty decent job getting most of it, but they're not allowed to go on private property. So how much of that can they encroach on before they've gone too far and the FEMA inspectors say, "You can't go any further?" People had their whole front yards filled with debris and then once it was picked up, there was a whole other load to come right behind that one.

Debris consisted of both natural and man-made things.
Harvey did not differentiate.
Photo courtesy of Patricia Vance

At one time, we probably had 12 or so trucks working here, but it wasn't enough. Then we had the CrowderGulf folks picking up debris, the city trucks picking up debris, and we got the state to come in and do some selected neighborhoods. All of which helped. But again, at the end of the day, it was the end of November before we got, say, 95% of the debris picked up. It couldn't be done fast enough.

Then you also had the church groups and other volunteer groups that went in and helped the individual families clean out, just to get their homes in some semblance of livable. Take the carpet out; take the sheet rock out; pile it all by the curb; muck out the home. All this went on while the homeowner waited for relief from the insurance company so they could put all that stuff back together.

And, unfortunately, I wouldn't say we had looters, but we had people who came through the neighborhoods and picked up flood-damaged stuff that people had placed out there. And if those things were your worldly possessions, and you saw people pick them up from the curb, it could be quite emotional. We had to deal with that at the same time.

We also had donations coming in and this was kind of one of the more interesting pieces. The Lions Club helped here. We loaded up a landscape trailer, an 8X12-foot or 16-foot landscape trailer, for example, and we just drove through neighborhoods and passed out cleaning supplies, water and paper products.

Eventually we just got so overrun that we got with Kroger and they gave us the old grocery store on FM 518. They gave it to us for a dollar. They sent their HVAC technician to get the AC back and operating. And then the Mayor, Ryan Smith and I put out a call for volunteers. The first day, we probably had a couple hundred volunteers. And then we got Carl Wankowicz as our "donation center manager." We were able to pay him -- not enough, but something. And he was there every day managing the donation center.

The first day we opened, we got two semis full of donations. And then throughout the day we probably got five or six more trucks of varying sizes, from a pickup truck pulling a trailer to a box truck. People all over the nation -- as far away as Georgia, as far north as Illinois, as far west as California – they just came. It varied from day to day. We did three, four, seven, eight trucks a day. The volunteers sorted it. They put it out. And it was gone every night.

The trucks were bringing in everything: clothing, shoes, water, food, baby supplies, cleaning supplies, new mattresses.

Kalpesh Patel, who owns the Hampton Inn and Candlewood Suites on I-45, brought 300 new mattresses to the donation center.

People brought food supplies for the volunteers. They never went hungry for lunch because somebody always dropped off something out there.

We got boxes of new shoes. Boxes and boxes. Probably ten pairs of all different tennis shoes. Bedding. More cleaning supplies. Hygienic supplies.

The grocery stores brought flats of bread, cases of bananas or other fruit, and pallets of water. I can't tell how many pallets of water I have moved.

We then collected hundreds of pallets in the back of the store. And hundreds of boxes from the food deliveries in the trash. So I got with our waste provider-- Republic -- and said, "Hey, I need a dumpster." We filled the dumpster up and there wasn't enough room, so we still had garbage and trash building up. So occasionally I'd jump in there and stomp it down, then fill it up again.

I called Republic and said, "Hey, we need another dumpster. Yeah, I don't care if you haul this one away, but give me another dumpster so I can manage trash."

That's all part of helping people. Not the glory part, rather a part that most people don't see.

So these volunteers collected the donations, sorted them and had a system to put them out. Then people came in every day, and they were able to pick up what they needed. Because there was only so much of each thing, we had to manage the amount of supplies each person or family got. But it was an interesting process.

We probably operated that for about 30 days. I was there every day for a while. I'd come to the office to work the day and then I'd go there from 6:00 to 9:00 pm to clean up and make sure everybody had what they needed. My wife was there, too, working with Carl most days to help any way she could.

And again, some people would just come by the center and others called beforehand. It was a tremendous outreach of the community to manage that center and the donations to help people who had just lost everything.

There were moms with babies who had nothing, their houses had been flooded or washed away. They were now living in apartments. They had nothing. I remember helping one teenage gentleman. The only thing he had were the clothes on his back and the same for his grandmother who was there with him. Because we had a lot of clothing donations, sometimes they weren't all out on display, so we went to the back of the Kroger store and started going through boxes just to find something for him to have so that he could return to school. So that's the type of things that we saw.

And then, of course, we had elected officials from all over the state: Dr. Bonnen, Senator Taylor, the Governor, and Senator Cruz all came.

I never would have envisioned running a shelter, feeding people, finding food, managing a donation distribution center and all the other tremendous needs with the clean-up of the community. It was an interesting time.

But I tell you, even today, there are homes out there that haven't been fully restored from all the Harvey damage. They've been made habitable. But people live there with four feet of their sheet rock out of the walls between rooms and stuff like that, because they didn't have insurance and they can't afford to fix them. That's tough.

The memories that still stick out in my mind are the times when I was able to interact with the community. The bird food was just one of those things. I think it was important for me to get out into the community and, for example, go to the grocery store. There were so many people who didn't leave before the storm and it was just hard to get stuff into the area for the first week or so afterwards. Then after that, things kind of smoothed out with the staff.

Rideaux Princeton was the name of the guy who was in the flooded dump truck who walked two or three miles back to Dickinson Avenue. He was also one of the first ones I saw when Esteban's opened up and provided him probably his first meal in 24 hours. Princeton just telling me the story about the flood and the logistical challenges he faced hit me hard.

I still think about the gentleman who flooded the truck trying to get Hometown Heroes open, who had to crawl through the window. I forget his name, but he was a pretty large guy. Thinking about him having to crawl out the window of the truck and fall into three- or four-foot-deep water. And Ryan Smith's story of driving past the truck and saying, "Oh my God, where is he? Did he get out or didn't he get out?" It sounds humorous today, but when it happened, it was horrible.

The other vivid memory I still have is around the donation distribution center, as I mentioned before, and just the hardship that people endured and the stories that they told you about their flooding: about what they were doing then and where they were living and what they needed. I hope I never see another Hurricane Harvey. I don't want to practice all I learned.

What would we do differently if we DID have another Harvey? I think we already responded differently than we have in the past. We had 48 inches of rain at Clear Creek. I think the question should be, "What can we do differently to make ourselves more resilient?"

We've done a number of things already. I used to say we should use a three-pronged attack, but I think I'm up to four prongs now. One of the things that the City Council did after was to step up our funding for maintenance. And we bought some new equipment, which will be very helpful in case of another storm.

We now mow major outfalls four times a year. Before it might have been a little more hit and miss. We try to keep the vegetation under control better now, so the water flows out better. Regular inspections on storm sewers and ditches and things like that. We enhanced our development standards.

Then what we call detention ponds used to have just a foot of freeboard, now they must have two feet of freeboard, so there's a higher safety factor.

There needs to be adjustments when we build new homes, too. We had about 8,000 homes impacted by flooding water. That's a lot. That was about 25% of the homes in the area. If we have another storm that bad, we want to prevent flooding before it happens. The old standard for rainfall was about 12 inches of rain in 24 hours. In new development, you have to design for the 500-year event. You have to design for what they call the "Atlas 14," which is about 50% more rainfall, so the new standard is 18 inches of rain in 24 hours.

We also work to manage how all that water is released downstream so it does no harm. Fixing drainage issues has been an iterative process. I can get all the engineers going, but it's still a long process to get through design iterations, etc. before that.

As you design, you find that some of it works, some of it perhaps impacts downstream. We evaluated that and enhanced our development standards. We enhanced our maintenance standards, focusing particularly on drainage in the hardest hit neighborhoods and the older subdivisions.

Think about Bay Ridge, about Dove Meadow, Oaks of Clear Creek, Bay Colony, and the Meadows. Most of those neighborhoods were built prior to detention standards. When the rain falls, it piles up in the streets, ultimately getting deep enough to go into the houses.

In 2019, the community supported a comprehensive drainage bond program. Two years after Harvey. Here we are in 2022, and some of those projects are underway. Bay Ridge, The Oaks of Clear Creek, Bay County are underway. In Dove Meadow, we just completed the land acquisition for the detention pond, so it'll probably be underway early in 2023. And The Meadows is a little bit further behind.

One of the things we try to do with those projects is take our local dollars and leverage them, where possible, for grant opportunities. The grantors look at what they call "cost benefit ratio." It means that we have to convince them that the benefit is higher than the cost. We felt that the Meadows project had a better chance to get a grant, so we sequenced it later in the process to accomplish that.

The other piece of this work involves all of the homes along the creek, which includes Clear Creek and -- to some extent -- Dickinson Bayou, because "what happens on the bayou" doesn't stay in the bayou. It goes up into drainage ditches until the water reaches a state of equilibrium. We started a collaborative effort with Galveston County, Harris County, the Army Corps of Engineers, Dickinson, Friendswood, Pearland, Brazoria County, Nassau Bay, Webster. I'm sorry if I forgot one. All of these communities participated in a regional study.

Ultimately, we know that the regional answer is some sort of a bypass tunnel – and its cost is about a billion dollars. We're struggling now with the question, "Do the benefits outweigh the cost?" We definitely don't want to see another Harvey. And if it's possible, we want to harden our communities from any future flooding.

Phase One of that study has been completed. We're working with the federal government, through the Army Corps of Engineers, to determine if there's a way to capture some of the ancillary benefits. For example, we can easily measure the $60,000 worth of damages in a house that was flooded, and there's X number of those in a flood event. What's harder to measure (and harder to defend) is, "Hey, my house is flooded and I'm a schoolteacher and I really can't get back to teaching school until I get my living stuff straightened out. Meanwhile, I lose my salary." So you lose dollars to the economy from that. Those kinds of damages are harder to measure monetarily.

The next piece of our study, and the Corps of Engineers has agreed to participate, is to make sure we capture all the ancillary damages so that we can defend the benefits we see from the project. This is a work in progress. It will not be accomplished in the immediate one-year or two-year timeframe, but we're continuing to work on it.

There are other issues, as well, such as "Can we reach a consensus in the community on what to do?" Clear Creek has been studied and looked at since least the '60s, if not before. But every project has aspects that benefit some and perhaps trouble others. Clear Creek remains kind of one of the last natural "creek/bayous" in the Houston area. Many of the creeks and bayous have been channelized and concreted. So there is obviously an environmental impact to making "improvements" to it.

In the ultimate analysis of Hurricane Harvey, I can definitely say that League City will be forever grateful for the unconditional assistance we received from the nation, from the church groups that came and helped people with their homes, from Kroger and HEB, from the restaurants that pitched in in the short term, from the folks at CrowderGulf.

Just the tenacity they all showed to keep going in spite of all the challenges. I couldn't be prouder of the staff members who worked side by side. The folks from Police and Fire and EMS and Public Works and Finance, and even the folks that weren't as directly involved, all stepped up to say, "Hey, what's my role in this?" That includes the folks from Helen Hall Library and the Recreation Department who manned the shelter at Hometown Heroes for weeks.

I forgot the folks from the Facilities Department. They answered the question, "Hey, the Devereux flooded and there's 125 people with nowhere to go -- right now -- today. What do I do?" I remember that we put them in the Civic Center for a few days. It was a rough few days because they didn't want to be there, but it was all we had to provide for them at the time.

I have tremendous gratitude and appreciation and, like I said, I'm proud of the folks that assisted. Everybody found a place where they could contribute the best. If they couldn't muck out houses, they went to the distribution center or they took food throughout the neighborhoods. It couldn't have been done without a total community effort. For that, I'm forever grateful.

I think League City, five years later, is well on its way to recovery, even though there's still work to do. We talked about the bond projects and bond programs to help make us more resilient to the next storm, because -- they all tell me -- there's another hurricane coming.

So to future generations, I say: It was awful to live through and if you can avoid a hurricane, avoid it. But if for some reason you're caught in a hurricane, or in any disaster, note that those experiences bring out the very best in people. It's neighbors helping neighbors. It's incredible. And we'll be there for you if something tragic like that happens again.

VII
You Never Know What You Are Going to Get
by Ogden "Bo" Bass, Assistant City Manager

The first I heard about a hurricane coming was a call I got on Friday morning, I think, that we needed to respond to the EOC (Emergency Operations Center) because the rain intensity and the rain bands were getting more involved.

I was hired for this position in June, and Harvey hit about two or three months later. Although I was born and raised in Freeport, Texas, and went through Carla there, it was still a bit of a rude awakening. I had been living in Dallas-Fort Worth for the past 25 years -- where it hardly ever rains.

I was lucky and was not personally affected by the storm. At the time, I was renting a little house in the Historic District, because I really like the old town. It's the highest elevation around. Why do you think the pioneers settled there...?

So when I got in my truck and started driving in, I noticed that the intersection of Coryell and Wisconsin was flooded. And I saw that Heritage Park was flooded, so I knew something was up as I rolled into the EOC.

For the most part, I found it already fully activated, but not yet fully staffed. People were starting to come in in spits and spurts because, again, at the time, it just looked like an unusually intense rainstorm event rather than what it later became.

We were absolutely not expecting the level of rainfall we eventually got. No. And I have the data. There are all kinds of numbers floating around, but this is a credible source, the Harris County Flood Control District: League City received 49.84 inches of rain in five days. I will tell you from personal experience, in our area, it actually took about three days to reach that level. That's over 4.1 feet of water!

What was interesting is the storm wasn't a wind event, okay? And it really wasn't a surge event where we are. I mean, it surged 3 to 3.5 feet along the coastal edge. So you take that 49.84 inches and add three feet on top of it, and that's how deep the water was right along the coast. It was nine feet in certain places. Some places had an inch in their houses: Some people had nine inches in their houses for four and five days. The poor people along Clear Creek, their homes were under water for days and days and days and days. So there you go.

Over four feet of rainfall resulted in water going wherever it wanted to -- and staying, sometimes for many days after the rain stopped falling.
Photo courtesy of C. Chapman

I had two principal functions. One was to find food because the storm intensified very, very quickly, and the roads flooded very, very quickly. We already had a contract in place with a company in Sugar Land to provide food under emergency circumstances, but they couldn't get here. And we had no provisions other than what we had in our duffle bags and that kind of thing. So in effect, we went back to the old school method: I got out the phone book, got on the phone and started calling every restaurant I could find.

The only restaurant I found that answered the phone that could help was Papa John's Pizza off FM 646. Go over the bridge from the office, it's on your left in a little strip center. So I called it and the manager answered and he said, "Hey, you know what? I'd love to help you, but I released all my staff about two hours ago when the water started coming out of the road. I'm trapped now and can't leave. But I'll tell you what. If you need it and it's for the city, I will fire up the ovens and I will bake every pizza I can." He effectively baked more than 80 pizzas for us.

Whatever the fellow's name is, which I can't remember, the manager of the Papa John's. Y'all need to go buy your pizzas at the Papa John's on FM 646. They still deserve that. They came across for us. Because our boys were hungry. I mean, Public Works had nothing. We were counting on trucks rolling in with mobile kitchens, with food supplies, ready to cook on site, and they couldn't get here. It was just like, "Okay, who has candy bars, and what do you have? I've got gum."

Now, how to get the pizzas. We figured out very quickly that the road on the Dickinson side of the FM 646 bridge was totally unpassable. So we had Pat Self, who at the time, I think, was Street Supervisor, get one of our dump trucks. We met him near the Chick-fil-A off FM 646. Pat took the big, high-water dump truck over the bridge. He went up and over, stopped, came back over, pulled up, and opened the door. All you could see was the top of Pat's head and as many Papa John's pizza boxes as you could possibly stuff into the cab. He made two trips. We transferred him and the pizzas into Jody's truck, and then we carried them not only to the EOC, but to Bauerschlag Elementary and a few other places and made deliveries. So kudos to that manager for coming across like that for us.

My second task for the day, in addition to acquiring provisions, was fuel recon. So I hooked up with Jody Hooks, the Director of Public Works, to get out into the field. Jody and I spent hours and hours going out into the field, verifying things and reporting back, "Yes, this is underwater…. Yes, this lift station is completely submerged…. Yes, this road is closed." That kind of thing.

My duties at that time were to get it all out of here and clean this place up. Also oversee any maintenance to wastewater, water supply, traffic signal operations, all those things. All the Public Works side. But I didn't do anything myself. I just helped kind of organize and direct.

My primary function was, again, making sure the water was clean and the pressures were good, the sanitary sewer systems worked and people had some comfort in their homes, that the traffic center worked and we didn't have wrecks, and then cleaning out all the debris.

I was more deeply and personally involved with CrowderGulf and another company called TetraTech to remove all the waste and debris. We ended up getting it done in about, I would say, maybe two and a half weeks. I mean, all said and done, it was really astounding. And this place was essentially clean in terms of all the tons and tons and tons of debris. I did a calculation one time on how many tons wet, how many tons dry, and it's in my folder in my file. I can't remember, but it was an astounding amount of material.

I did a lot of coordinating where we triaged, around which neighborhoods were hit the hardest, which neighborhoods should be dealt with first, those kinds of things. It was a coordination based on the private contract we had in place prior to the storm with CrowderGulf. They rolled their forces in. We had TexDOT come in and do a couple of neighborhoods on the west side. And then our Public Works crews filled in some gaps on emergencies when people just absolutely were in desperate straits and the situation was too small for the big contractors. So we would go in and do it ourselves.

Another part of the story. Jody and I were sitting at one of our recon points in an absolutely driving rain. If you were born on the Gulf Coast, you've been through this kind of rain. It's like the most intense squall you've ever seen, but nonstop.

I looked over to my right, which was westward, I think, and all of the main lanes on I-45 were flooded. I-45 was totally shut down. And there were people kayaking down the middle of the interstate. It's true.

Probably the most stirring moment for me was when we were sitting there on the opposite side of the bridge. A family came walking across the bridge in the driving rain. They literally were walking out of Dickinson because they had lost their home. They walked like ducklings.

They had umbrellas and luggage, but no rain gear. They looked like refugees. And it was a mom and a dad and two kids, maybe three, I can't remember. But it was just really poignant to watch them go over the bridge, seeking succor and support in League City because they had lost their home. And they were evacuating by foot. It was that bad.

During the height of the event, Dickinson sent out a formal emergency text and I'll paraphrase it. It said something like, "From the City of Dickinson. If you have not evacuated as of this moment, we will not be able to rescue you."

That was incredible. I'd never imagined I'd see something like that except for war time or something. But it was that bad: Cities were denying rescue because they couldn't send their forces out.

The City of League City did the best we could. Absolutely. We had police officers who were skilled in high-water rescue out there in dump trucks with our Public Works drivers because police officers couldn't drive dump trucks and our boys in the dump trucks couldn't do the high-water rescues.

They went into as many locations as they could and helped people get into these dump trucks. But there were places the dump trucks couldn't go. It was so bad.

I remember the Mayor has said this over and over again. He remembers looking out his window and seeing a Public Works truck full of little old ladies and men being taken out. Otherwise, God knows what would've happened to them.

So yes, Public Works was fully engaged, with Fire, Police, EMS, and to a smaller extent, Parks and Recreation. We have over 170 lift stations and, if they go down with the kind of water volumes we were getting, and if the plant stops operating, everything that goes in those sewer pipes goes back into our homes. So we were racing everywhere to address emergencies because the power grid had gone down. We were running around, hooking up, pumping down the sumps, and moving from station to station. Managing the human waste. Because if we didn't, it was going to float off or push back up, overpressure, and go back into people's houses.

There were lift stations that, quite frankly, were totally inundated. The bridge over Clear Creek on (I think) Bay Area.... Literally once you cleared that curve, it was completely under water all the way across near where Countryside Park is. And there were boats traveling all up and down the roads. It was wild.

I still think that one of the most important things that happened in our favor was Pat Self bringing the pizzas, because that was critical. Other than that, all we had was potato chips and Cokes. Since then, there have been great lessons learned and now we have made provision for emergencies.

Another thing that stuck in my mind is that we had a critical lift station that was almost completely underwater at Lynn Gripon Park at Countryside. The wet wells of the station were in danger of being overtopped. We had to pump the thing.

Remember, this is all under water. It's not clear like a bathtub. The electrician literally followed the power cables down, standing in the water, to make the connection so we could make sure the lift station worked. Dangerous work, but it needed to be done, and he volunteered to do it. So he stood out in my mind.

Jody Hooks and I did a lot of the field work. John, the City Manager, had to be stationed there because he's the head of the EOC in that kind of circumstance. He was able to see reports on all the major news networks. He was also getting errant reports from citizens and from police officers.

So John would say, "Hey, I want to know about this location. Go put eyes on it." So we'd go out there and put eyes on it and come back and report or call in.

One more flood story: We were driving down -- I don't remember what road it was -- in Jody's truck. It was one of the westside subdivisions. And again, the water was just as high as can be. Water was completely up to the fence edges. And as we're going slow and driving through, we noticed the top of something in the middle of the green space.

I said, "What is that?"

Jody said, "It's a pickup truck."

It seemed that somebody thought they knew a smart way to get around the deeper water and decided to jump the curb, go up into the HOA open space – where they thought it was shallower --and just proceed from there.

What they didn't realize is that there was a pond there that was already three feet underwater. They didn't see it and drove right into it.

Regarding aftereffects, the most striking memory I have was in the Park on Clear Creek. We were going through, and the residents were completely overrun with water. Essentially, every possession they had on the first floor of their homes was out in their front yards. It was astounding. It was like Galveston after Rita or Ike. There were piles of furniture and art and carpet and freaking televisions and just all kinds of... just everything you could imagine. Just piles of it taller than people. All through this subdivision.

I also remember Jody and I were going slow around the neighborhoods taking photos of everything, and we saw a kitchen sink fly up and hit the top of a pile of debris. We looked at each other, "What the heck?"

So we stopped and got out to look, and there's a woman who's literally ringed by this circle of her own personal property which had to be eight feet tall. She's in the middle, crying, and stacking additional materials on top of it all.

We asked, "Is there anything we can do?"

And she said, "No."

So we kept on going. But that was pretty striking for us.

So now that we can look back from a distance, would we do anything different? Yes. Absolutely. We had multiple after-action reports, and we now have different kinds of contract procedures in place for pumps and generators and for food supplies, and we've stockpiled a bunch of materials, water supplies and those kinds of things. So yeah, it was a learning moment for us.

A classic quote is that "no plan survives first contact with the enemy." We thought we were prepared. And we were for a classic event like Rita, like Ike. More of a "trees are down and power's down" kind of event. We were not prepared for the type of rivering inundation that we had in Harvey. So it adjusted our thinking, no question about that.

Another thing we learned. Just do exercises. Plan for A, B, C, and D, and just keep at it and keep training, period. Because the reality is whatever you train for, you're going to get something slightly different. But if you've trained, at least you will be nimble enough to respond more effectively, hopefully.

After all, you never know what you're going to get.

VIII
Hurricanes Haunt Our History
by Joyce Zongrone, USN (Ret.)

We have learned that powerful hurricanes have historically pounded ancient lands from the first millennium (during the peak of the Roman Empire) through the height of the Middle Ages and beyond.

We have records of two early hurricanes that occurred in August 1508. The first of these storms forced Ponce de Leon's ship onto the rocks in Hispaniola. Two weeks later, the second storm beached his vessel on the southwest coast of Puerto Rico. In September 1565, another major hurricane scattered a French fleet near Jacksonville, Florida.

A maritime archaeological study done by Woods Hole Oceanographic Institution (WHOI) in Massachusetts was the first to find evidence and remains of 32 prehistoric hurricanes, along with two documented ones that occurred in 1635 and 1675 on the east coast of the US.

Texas, too, is no stranger to dangerous storms. The first recorded major storm in Texas was in 1527, which sank the ship of Spanish conquistador Panfilo de Narváez off the coast of Galveston Island and killed 200 of his men.

Nature did not even spare the infamous pirate Jean Laffite. In 1818, a hurricane nearly wiped out his colony of 2,000 people. Survivors sought refuge in his home, Maison Rouge, which had been built on the highest point on the island. The site of his home exists today on Harborside Drive, between 14th and 15th streets.

The most devastating natural disaster in US history was a

hurricane that leveled Galveston in 1900, resulting in the loss of 6,000 to 8,000 lives. It is still considered our nation's greatest natural disaster.

Most recently, Hurricane Harvey set several records for tropical cyclones in the US, including rainfall, storm surge, devastating winds and flooding.

This book is a primary source for accounts of those who endured Hurricane Harvey and survived. The stories included here represent and underscore the human drama as the storm unfolded, and it celebrates our human resiliency. Harvey will be forever etched in our collective memory.

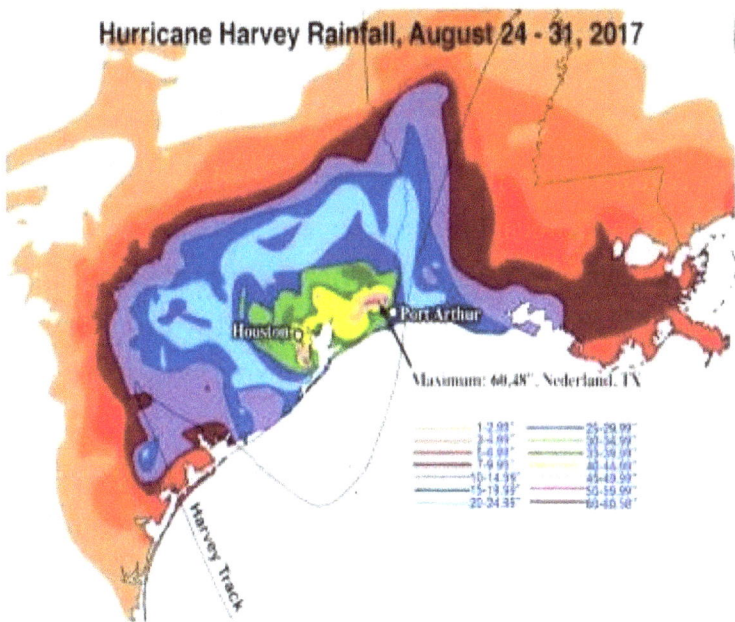

Photo courtesy of the National Weather Service of Houston/Galveston

IX
Eye on the Storm: The National Weather Service
By Joyce Zongrone, USN (Ret.)

Long before Hurricane Harvey entered the consciousness of League City residents, the Houston/Galveston Forecast Office of the National Weather Service (NWS) had its eye on the Gulf. The NWS has operated its weather observation and forecasting program for 152 years, since 1870, when Congress authorized the Army Signal Corps to aid in reducing loss of life and property damage from major weather events.

For four days prior to landfall, Dan Reilly, Warning Coordinator Meteorologist, a 29-year veteran of the NWS, tracked Harvey and briefed county officials and the US Coast Guard.

According to Reilly, the storm turned out to be exactly what the NWS had forecasted.

It "was a very rare case where a record rainfall event was forecast with confidence," Reilly said. "It was hard for people to visualize, since it was outside their experience, and some didn't feel like it applied to them."

Harvey set a record for rainfall amount of five feet (that's 60 inches!) near Nederland, Texas. The storm also set a record for tropical cyclones in the United States. At landfall, it was a Category 4 storm, producing six- to ten-foot storm surges with winds of 130 miles per hour. The storm also set records for catastrophic flooding and multiple fatalities.

Dan Reilly, Warning Coordinator Meteorologist,
National Weather Service of Houston/Galveston,
was at his console during Hurricane Harvey.
Photo courtesy of the National Weather Service of Houston/Galveston

X
Why Dickinson Floods
by Harvey Cappel, P.E.

I'm not picking on Dickinson, but simply using it to tell why some places flood and others don't. During Hurricane Harvey, Dickinson flooded and sustained damage to nearly every building. Texas City, on the other hand, had minimal flooding from the same storm. Why?

The first reason you hear about is elevation. Although higher elevation can be a benefit, it is no guarantee. Denver, Colorado, has suffered flooding from heavy rainfall. And, on the other hand, Tiki Island and Bayou Vista, both only a few feet in elevation, had no flooding caused by rainfall during Harvey.

Before getting technical, let's define the flooding we are concerned with here: It's rising water due to *rainfall*. Tidal surge and high tides can be factors in flooding, but the intense rainfall of Harvey was, in this case, the big problem.

Rainfall flooding is about drainage and not absolute elevation. You can suffer flooding at any elevation if the water is coming down faster than it can drain away. You might not think so but being very close to Galveston Bay is the best way you can avoid rainfall flooding. The rainwater can get to the "big pond" (Galveston Bay) very quickly and the pond is big enough that its level will not rise due to the addition of rainwater.

Not since Noah loaded up the Ark has rainfall raised the water in large bays and oceans: They are too vast to be affected by rainfall.

This street view is an excellent example that rainfall flooding is all about drainage rather than total rainfall amount.
Photo courtesy of C. Chapman

Dickinson flooded because it has an inadequate drainage system (for the "Harvey" rate of rainfall) and Texas City did not flood because it does have a good enough drainage system. Other areas, including much higher elevations than Dickinson, flooded for the same reason. Their drainage systems could not drain the water faster than it was coming down.

So let's take a technical look at the Dickinson drainage system. Dickinson includes an area of about ten square miles and has basically only one water highway to the Gulf of Mexico -- that being Dickinson Bayou. I did some rough (I mean really rough) calculations and found that Dickinson Bayou cannot even handle a one-half-inch-per-hour continuous rainfall from just half of the city area. And I have no idea what the other half has as a drainage system.

Drainage systems always work in the long run by having the upstream elevation of the water high enough for it to flow downstream to the big pond. Unfortunately, in the case of Dickinson, this rise in water elevation cannot be achieved without the water getting out of the water highway (Dickinson Bayou), so the water spreads out everywhere until it is high enough to make the drainage system work.

This, of course, is the cause of the flooding. When we have a high tide and/or hurricane surge, this in-town water elevation must go up enough to keep the elevation difference the same. This allows the water to flow to the big pond as fast as it is coming down.

Texas City has implemented a strategy to use pumps and an intermediate pond (Moses Lake) to artificially force the drainage required. Dickinson's solution: increase the width of Dickinson Bayou and add some drainage canals.

XI
A Hurricane Like No Other
by R. M. Shepherd

In the week prior to its arrival, we watched the news about the coming hurricane, which had been named Harvey. This was not our first hurricane, as I have lived in Houston for over 40 years and my husband for over 50 years. We are both senior citizens. Each storm has taught us different lessons, and we try to use those lessons for the next storm. During Hurricane Ike in 2008, we lost electricity for ten days and learned what supplies to store up to get through another possible electrical outage. We now have a "storm box," a large gray plastic container in which we keep our hurricane supplies.

When we heard that Harvey was headed to the Gulf Coast, we went into action. Days ahead of time, we collected extra water and food that was canned or dry. In case we lost electricity, we had batteries for flashlights and radios, and candles, lamps, and lamp oil. We filled up our vehicles because gasoline had been scarce after Hurricane Ike. We also charged our cell phones, remembering that much of the news post-Ike was on the websites of the major stations, and at the time neither of us had a "smart phone."

Even with all the preparations, we were still uneasy because we had moved from inside Loop 610 in Houston to League City just over three years before, and our house and subdivision had been built "post Ike." Our neighbors had not been through a hurricane, so they – and now we -- did not know what to expect.

It started raining on Friday, August 25, and continued most

of the night and the next day. But we remained cautiously optimistic. The water was draining off our lot and into the storm sewers. Harvey was on track to make landfall in Port Aransas, so we did not expect hurricane-force winds. The weather forecasters were predicting several days of rain, possibly as much as 24 inches. But we thought we would be OK.

We lost power early on Saturday and started preparations for using our supplies. Thankfully, Texas/New Mexico Power restored the electricity in less than two hours.

So all day Saturday we stayed glued to the TV, which reported flooding in many parts of the Gulf Coast. Nervously, we checked the street and the backyard often, but the water was still draining. Eventually, there was street flooding, but none in our yard -- yet.

That evening, the tornado warnings began. Since the tornadoes were moving about 30 miles per hour when they touched down, we spent the night in the safest room in our house—my walk-in closet. We cleared out the boxes and shoes on the floor and borrowed cushions from the sofa to put down for sleeping.

We tried to keep our dog in there with us, but she would not stay. She is afraid of thunder, so a few months previously I had bought her a "Thundershirt™" which is used to calm pets down when they are nervous. I put the garment on her and had to leave it on all night.

The idea of sleep that night was optimistic! The tornado alerts came frequently and, just as one expired, another would take its place. We dozed off but could not fully sleep.

In the meantime, the rain grew heavier, and we left our "safe room" periodically to see how high the water had risen. It started coming up onto the lawn, but not very high, so we went back to the "safe room." We checked periodically throughout the night.

Flood line at the sidewalk of R.M. Shepherd's house during Hurricane Harvey
Photo courtesy of R. M. Shepherd

The tornado alerts finally ended in the early morning. We looked outside in the daylight and saw that the water had been over the curb and almost halfway up into our lawn, leaving a trail of debris when it receded. The flooding had washed the dirt from around the roots of our rose bush near the street, leaving a large clump of dirt and mulch nearby.

We called family and friends in the area to determine how they were doing. Aside from minor roof leaks, everyone was dry and safe. Our oldest daughter and her husband had rescued an elderly couple who attend their church because their house in Friendswood had flooded.

Sunday morning, because of street flooding, our church in Clear Lake was closed. But our senior pastor held a quick service on Facebook Live. We connected to it and joined him in his prayers for all who were adversely affected. We checked on our neighborhood Facebook page and learned that most houses were safe, although all the roads surrounding the subdivision were flooded.

And it was still raining, although not as hard.

As Sunday ended and then Monday dawned, it was still raining, but the storm sewers continued to carry the water away.

The flooding in surrounding communities was worse, and we discovered that the bank in Dickinson where we have a safe deposit box had flooded. The box holds keepsakes from my father and brother who passed in the 1980's. Many years ago, I had a safe deposit box in the tunnel system in downtown Houston when the tunnels flooded. That bank did not flood, but I have enclosed my items in plastic since then. So naturally we were worried about how high the water was in the Dickinson bank. Streets surrounding the bank remained flooded for several days, so we could not check.

The rain finally stopped, and the sun came out. What a relief for those affected by the flood waters. We waited until the following week to get more groceries since my husband had prepared well. Many stores were closed or allowed only a few people in at a time to shop and, although we waited, the local stores were still out of bread. They were quickly restocking fresh fruit and vegetables, but it would be another week or more before we could buy the bread and buns that we normally use.

Empty bread shelves at a store in the
aftermath of Hurricane Harvey
Photo courtesy of C. Chapman

My husband began the ordeal of calling about the status of the bank and had to make many calls. We discovered there had been three feet of water in the bank, and it would be weeks before they would let the customers examine their safe deposit boxes for damage. We continued to worry about water damage and mold during those weeks.

Finally, bank personnel moved the boxes to a dry location at another branch and we were able to access our box. Thankfully, there was no water and no mold.

Although we were mostly spared, every time it rains heavily now, I check to see if the water is rising in the street. Other lessons we learned:

- Stock up on bread
- Pack a – waterproof -- "to-go bag" with clean clothes and shoes
- Pack some food, water and medication
- And pack a bag for your dog, as well!

XII
Gracie's Boat Ride
by R. M. Shepherd

Gracie woke and perked up her ears. It was Sunday morning, August 27, 2017. The rain had begun two days before, and dull gray clouds covered the sky. She could hear the rain falling on the deck, but she was hungry and needed to go outside.

Gracie is a Labradoodle who loves the water and spends hours swimming. She stood up, shook herself, and started looking for her parents Dave and Nancy. When she found them, she let them know she needed to go outside. Nancy walked with her to open the door to the outside and Gracie started to go through.

But she hesitated; something was wrong. Where was the grass? All she could see in all directions was water! And it was dirty and had an unpleasant odor.

Dave, Nancy and Gracie live on a street in Harris County that slopes down toward Clear Lake. Their waterfront house is elevated from the street and, in the past, has never flooded.

As Gracie hesitated at the door, Dave and Nancy looked at each other and at the water and expressed their surprise. They knew that a hurricane had been forecast and, as long-time residents on the Gulf Coast, they had made the usual precautions: food, fresh water, batteries, etc. They had also moved as much as they could from the first floor to the second in case the water came into their house.

But Hurricane Harvey was different. They had never seen so much rain before, and the water on their street had never been this deep during the time they had lived there.

They turned on the TV but listening to the news was discouraging: The forecast was for continued rain for several days.

The water already covered the street and most of their lawn. Water was already in the houses across the street. And it already covered the cars that had been left in the street to their roof tops— all of which meant there was more than five feet of water out there.

The water had reached the tops of the cars.
A white square is all that is visible of a flooded
pick-up truck on a street in Friendswood.
Photo courtesy of Gary Macdonell

With only a tiny patch of grass in sight in their yard, Gracie went back into the house. Dave and Nancy discussed the problem: Gracie needed to find an area of grass large enough for her to use. Then Dave exclaimed, "I'm going to take Gracie in the kayak!"

He knew that there was dry land nearby, and the kayak was shallow and maneuverable enough that he could go through the flooded roads to reach it. But it was still raining, and Gracie hated the rain. She has a raincoat, boots, and a hat to keep the rain off when they walk her, but that did not help with flood waters.

Dave went outside to where the kayak was stored and carried it to the front of the house. He secured it while Nancy brought Gracie out. The dog was nervous, so Nancy found Gracie's favorite ball and put it in the kayak. Gracie loves her ball and was now eager to get into the kayak with Dave.

They helped her into the kayak, then released the lines and Dave paddled away. He thought about the Biblical flood and Noah's search for dry ground. He was pretty sure that it wouldn't take too long to find grass.

The current was strong, however, and Dave had to concentrate on paddling to steer it in the direction they needed to go. Gracie was happily playing with her ball when suddenly she picked it up and dropped it into the water.

Dave watched in alarm as Gracie jumped into the dirty water after the ball.

Dave then leaped into the water to rescue Gracie.

He was a tall man, and the water was chest deep. The current was strong, and he was at least half a mile from a safe place to secure and board the kayak. Pulling the kayak and leading Gracie, he struggled toward dry land.

Dave spotted a dry patch of ground and the grass, green and wet, beckoned. When they reached higher ground, Gracie was excited and ran across the grass. Ah! Mission accomplished! She continued to sniff and pace and enjoy being on the grass again.

Soon, however, Dave called her to get back into the kayak and they headed home. When they arrived, Nancy helped Gracie back into the house, and Gracie headed for a well-earned nap.

Dave repeated this journey with their pet several times during and after the storm. Dave also used his kayak to help his neighbors who had flooded homes.

XIII
Harvey: First Hurricane
by Wali Muhammad

I've seen many stories on television about "evacuees" and my policy has always been, "rather see one, than be one." That policy ended abruptly in September 2017, with the arrival in Texas of one hurricane named Harvey.

CNN reported that Harvey dumped an estimated 27 trillion gallons of rain over Texas and Louisiana during a six-day period, according to a weather analytics company named WeatherBell. The rainfall set a record as the "most ever" from a tropical cyclone as it "made landfall" in the continental US.

Welcome to Texas. We've been here going on five years now and this was our first hurricane.

"AWAAANK!, AWAAANK!," squawked the phone, demanding our attention. Warning! Warning!

I looked at my wife and tapped the screen on the phone. "Hurricane, Shmurricane! How bad can this be? It's even named after a comedian."

As I spoke those words in jest, memories from the Hurricane Preparedness seminar that we had attended began creeping in. So I bravely told my wife, "It's all in the leaving, the staying and the returning. We got this! I'll work through Friday, and we'll take off for Austin."

Leaving! That's no problem. We've driven to Austin dozens of times. It's a straight shot -- airport to airport – Hobby to Bergstrom. Got that covered.

Staying! No problem. We have grown children there with

houses. We kick back, get to spend some time with the grandkids.

Returning! No problem. We'll just keep in touch with the neighbors and come back when all is clear.

Our house is on 16-foot pilings and, according to the medallion on the tree in the front yard, the height of the water from Hurricane Ike -- a profoundly damaging storm -- was only eight feet. But…that is actually higher than the fence and motorized gate we had installed.

Uh-oh…. We now have the first sign of potential trouble. The company that installed the gate told us that, in event of anticipated flooding, they would come out and remove the circuit board and batteries from the unit and we could still roll the gate manually. It's a few days ahead of Harvey's arrival, so I call. But no answer on their phone.

We began gathering and checking the items "necessary" for our getaway: Water, blankets, extra food. "Hey," I said, "it's only to Austin…a couple hours' drive at the most. And we're not anticipating a direct hit. Landfall is expected to the south and west."

"Wait," my wife said. "Doesn't that put us on the 'dirty side' of the storm?"

Still no call-back from the fence guy.

And what about the other car and the golf cart? Should we park them at the Home Depot lot – where we've seen emergency vehicles staging during previous storms? Seems to be "higher ground."

That may be alright for the car, but the golf cart is another story, it's not as secure because they all seem to run off the same key. However -- there's a friend in Clear Lake Shores with a garage who has helped us once before when we lost charge during the island-wide garage sale. Let's call about leaving the golf cart there.

"No problem" was the response, right off. But later came a return call with second thoughts. "Perhaps," he said, "it's best not to leave it here." We then thought about using jack stands to raise it off the ground and leave it under the house.

Another day came with more warnings, "but no need to evacuate Houston," the administration said.

Well, it's still our first hurricane and we're leaving...no question. Just a little later than we thought. Tomorrow should be fine.

Then came a desperate call from our youngest son, "LEAVE NOW!" He reminded us of his own horror stories when evacuating ahead of Hurricane Rita in 2005. He was living in Houston at the time, and we were still in Georgia. It was shortly after Katrina, and everyone took the warnings seriously – and everyone left at the same time. He reminded us of his desperate phone calls to Georgia while stuck in gridlock for two days trying to evacuate. He reminded us that more people died in the evacuation turmoil than perished during the storm itself.

We decided then and there to leave early. But wait.... Still no callback from the fence company about the circuit board on the gate mechanism. Finally, once we were on the road, the fence company called to say they were not able to remove the board, but "I know a guy, used to work for me, perhaps he can do it...."

He called back later and agreed to remove the circuit board for a credit card payment over the phone. To top it off, he charged double to put it back after the storm.

XIV
Hurricane Harvey Observations
by Mike Conwell

Sunday, August 27

We awoke at 7:00 am. The power had gone off at 12:30 am with a huge lightning strike. I got up and went to the front door in my stocking feet and felt water in the carpet. The water had come in the front door and into the front rooms. I told my wife Pat and then started the gas refrigerator in our trailer to move some of our food out there.

My son Mike put together a family text network with the five of us. He was watching Transtar cameras and bayou levels from Austin. He said that League City had gotten 14.4 inches of rain in the night.

Our rain gauge had maxed out. The water I saw out the front door was Clear Creek. There were no whirlpools above the drains, which meant that nothing was draining.

Later in the day, I found 23 inches of water in a trash can in the yard. That was close to what the news programs had indicated. We listened to KUHF on the radio every couple of hours. Our neighbor from across the street knocked on the door and said that he still had power and that we were welcome to it. I said maybe, after the water had gone down in the street.

Pat and I went for a walk in the afternoon, but Pat stopped at Rondel, saying that the water was too deep. I continued to Landrum Lane where I found a group of neighbors collected around an ATV. They offered me a beer and it really hit the spot. I went on until the water was up to my thighs and decided to turn around. Pat was waiting in the driveway, and I took a picture of her.

Pat Conwell awaits her husband's return to their home after
wading out through the deep, muddy water.
Photo courtesy of Mike Conwell

Our neighbor showed up at the door with a power cord around five and we routed it through the front window in order to plug in the refrigerator. Later, we plugged in the TV center, a lamp and a spot for the phone chargers.

We watched the TV coverage in the evening. Channel 11 KHOU had to evacuate their studios on Allen Parkway. They fell back to using a kitchen table and laptop computers and partnered with KXAA Channel 8 in Austin (even though it's ABC) to keep broadcasting. Their stringers were manning trouble points around the city.

Monday, August 28

We slept well because the room was so dark. The streetlight provided a little light. The water level had gone down in the night, so we took a half-mile walk in a light rain as far as Landrum, where the water covered the sidewalk.

When we returned, I took the car out of the garage and got the wet/dry vacuum ready to use. I vacuumed the garage and half-filled the bucket by noon, when we broke for lunch and a nap. We charged our phones while we slept.

The road was covered with water by the time we woke up, but we were determined to look for bananas at Kroger. It wasn't a smart move because the intersections are deeper than the road by our house. Kilgore's was closed and Kroger's was just closing at 4:00 pm We stopped at Dollar General and bought three plastic containers to organize and keep papers and records dry. Our son Peter brought us a hundred cardboard boxes later on, just in case.

My nephew called later in the day, and we were also able to talk to our daughter on the phone. They wanted to come help when the roads were clear, but they were impassable just then. I also called my brother, but he was at dinner with friends in Ellicottville (he had been golfing for two days).

I put four hot dogs on the grill, finished my supper and called my brother again. It's good that he had seen our house in the rain.

I got lost in watching the coverage in the evening. There was a flood of volunteers helping out with their boats. One group was the Cajun Navy. BSI had fielded two of their huge articulated dump trucks in SW Houston so they could haul 50 people at a time away from flooded areas. The Army Corps of Engineers was releasing water into Buffalo Bayou from Addick's and Barker reservoirs. One reservoir was at 104 feet.

Hilton Furniture was moving people to Walmart for transfer to the George R. Brown Convention Center. The center was at capacity at 5000 people, but the mayor said "Forget capacity. No one will be turned away."

The KPRC reporter was getting exasperated by the absence of government people at his station under an overpass. He was told that the Coast Guard was prohibited from working after dark. They had extended their limits but took the night off.

One final surprise from Galveston -- Scholes Field was still operational, and the Texas National Guard had already flown 400 people to Dallas. Who knew? I went to bed after that.

Tuesday, August 29

We awoke at seven the next morning and soon got a call from our son Mike. Breaking news: The Brazos River had breached the levee at Columbia Lakes, and they were evacuating. Water was flowing over the spillway at Addick's Reservoir. ABC News was concentrating on Baytown where water was up to the roofs.

Anyway, Mike called to say that Clear Creek was up 2½ feet. I looked out the window and, sure enough, the water was up to the trailer again. I-45 was closed from Clear Creek to El Dorado Boulevard. I decided to catch up on my journal and then get back to vacuuming up the water. There were now 9000 people at the GRB and Dallas said they had 6000 beds available at their convention center. The Toyota Center was also being fitted out so people could be moved there.

We watched a heart-stopping rescue of two men on I-90 East. A man was clinging to a sign and got the attention of a reporter about a hundred feet away. The reporter thought he was the driver of a blue container truck that was now submerged.

Another man began swimming toward him, but then the first man swam out of sight as an Army helicopter circled overhead. The helicopter lowered a rescue diver to pick him up, but the diver returned empty handed. Maybe the fellow thought it was too dangerous to be raised when they were close to the power lines. A boater heard about the situation and arrived to complete the rescue of both men.

We took a break to eat lunch and nap.

The TV coverage is so fascinating that it's hard to break away from it. A 20-vehicle convoy arrived in Angleton from NYPD and NYFD.

Judge Ed Emmett announced that the NRG Center was opening as a 10,000-bed refuge, and Judge Eckels and Mayor White were tapped to be in charge of the operation. Baker-Ripley would be managing it. Houston Livestock & Rodeo Association volunteers were also going to work it since NRG is their building. It would include 200 volunteers, a pet area, children's area, dining hall, HEB Store, medical services and more. Judge Emmett predicted that it would be half full by morning.

We ate ham and eggs for supper again and went for a walk after the dishes were finished. We met a neighbor and two of her dogs.

The water in Clear Creek was level with the Butler Longhorn Museum parking lot now. As we approached our driveway, the spotlights on the outside of the house came on. I was taken aback, wondering how that could be. Did I put a battery back-up on them? Of course, I didn't! The power was back on! I happily sent a text message to tell the family.

Wednesday, August 30

Was it just last night that the lights came back on? I thought of the water rescue story yesterday and the joke usually told by ministers:

Flood survivor: "God, why did you leave me in the water like that when I prayed for relief?"

God: "I sent you a big strong Romanian man to help you, but you swam away. I sent you a helicopter to drop you a line, but you waived off the rescue diver. I sent you a bunch of Cajuns in a boat and you climbed aboard."

The Marines brought 14 of their Assault Amtracks from Galveston to Friendswood. These are big, scary, tracked vehicles.

Our Twitter and Podcast services had stopped but the City finally sent a letter this evening saying that we will have to wait until Monday for trash service and another week for recycling.

I took our neighbor's extension cord back to his garage. We were able to go to the Post Office, Kilgore's, and Kroger's. I went through the high water where the Heritage Park Pond went across Coryell. The level of the water was down by our afternoon walk but it was awfully muddy.

We continued to watch the news reports. We saw an amazing picture of US-59 where the river had pushed the concrete barriers across the freeway in a gigantic question mark. At another spot, workers had installed an inflatable barrier alongside the roadway to keep Buffalo Bayou from overflowing onto the road. Military helicopters also evacuated residents from a flooded nursing home in Beaumont to a facility in Conroe.

We learned of a tragedy that occurred a couple of days ago when a man tried driving through deep water to cross Greens Bayou. His van was swept off the road. He was able to get out of his window and cling to a tree, but he left four children and their grandparents in the van. The van and their bodies were found this morning. Surviving family members discovered the van. Two police chaplains were there with the family, giving their support.

This pile of bricks is under the intersection of I-45 and FM 517, the victim of the same surging floodwaters as in this story.
Photo courtesy of C. Chapman

Arkema Chemical Company uses really dangerous chemicals as feedstock for organic peroxide that is used in plastic products. Their plant in Crosby lost primary power as well as backup power which is used to cool these unstable compounds. Residents in a mile-and-a-half radius of the plant have been evacuated. The company believes that the chemicals will burn or explode within the next six days.

By this time, the water level in Heritage Pond was down to street level at Coryell Street, so kayakers could put their boats right in the water from the road.

Jim McIngvale opened the Gallery Furniture showroom as a shelter, so people were sleeping in $2000 beds and $999 lounge chairs. There were soldiers billeted there, also.

My daughters Susan and Jenny, who live in San Antonio, got together at a Home Depot store there and called us to see what we needed. They were buying and renting supplies that were out of stock in the Houston area.

Thursday

As was feared, there was a small explosion at Arkema today.

We made a big decision today when we went back to look at "Dead Man's Curve" and saw all of the wet carpeting spread out on Moody Street. While I had been vacuuming the wet carpet, I hadn't been factoring in the padding under the carpet. You can dry the carpet out all you want but when you walk on it, the water is going to squeeze up from the padding.

We also learned today that there was a change in the law affecting the speed that insurance claims are processed, and that it was going into effect against homeowners the next day. We went to see our State Farm agent Steve. He came out to greet us and told us that if the carpet is wet, it has to come up. Steve's assistant Amanda made a claim to the NFIP for us. She entered our address, phone number and email address and we were done. They will call or email a claim number. We came home and texted the kids as to the change of plans.

We checked Whataburger again, but they were still closed. We ate lunch and napped. My nephew in Florida called us late in the afternoon to see how we were.

After a nap, I moved the photo albums to coolers in the garage to protect them. We decided to go to Red River Barbecue for supper so we could buy a $25 gift card for our neighbor to thank him for the electricity. I called the restaurant ahead of time and was told that they were out of brisket and pulled pork. I had a stuffed potato with sausage and Pat had a hamburger. We visited with our neighbor to give him the gift card and talked for 20 minutes. He told us that the propeller had blown off his windmill during the hurricane.

ABC ran a telethon today to collect money for the Red Cross. Sandra Bullock donated a million dollars to the Texans' JJ Watts' fund. He donated a million dollars and set a goal of $10 million for hurricane relief. I listened to more podcasts than TV today.

Jenny and Susan arrived around 9:30 with a load of stuff. They brought three rented carpet fans and dehumidifiers from our sons Peter and Mike. There were extension cables, a saw, trash bags (paper and plastic) and a little bit of luggage.

Help had arrived! And more would come tomorrow.

XV
Alligator!
By Rob Armstrong
(as told to Patricia Vance)

As soon as the receded flood waters had made streets passable, the residents flocked into the neighborhood to survey the state of affairs in their waterlogged houses. Several people had congregated to talk, share shocked emotions, cry, console, express disbelief that such an unexpected thing had happened, offer encouragement, and try to map out a recovery plan -- just to name a few topics.

Rob Armstrong was in this crowd of men who were swapping flood stories. His house had 18 inches of nasty water in it, but at the end of the block, the water was only three to four feet deep in the street and it had not gotten into the houses.

One neighbor told a story he had heard from another neighbor. It goes like this:

A father and his 10-year-old daughter were wading through a section of water that was waist-deep and chest-deep (respectively), trying to escape to high and dry ground. Each of them was carrying a much-loved pet dog.

All of a sudden, the father saw something long and slim floating about six feet ahead of them. It was coming closer at a smooth, steady glide. His first thought was a tree log, since so many downed limbs were everywhere. But as it got closer, he could see what it really was.

Father and daughter both froze and held their breath. The "it" was looking straight forward, which was actually excellent news as the two were perpendicular to the intruder.

Quick thinking and good common sense prevailed. Being the good protective dad that he was, he whispered, "If the head turns to us, throw the dog!"

Thankfully the "swimming log" with a snout and bulging eyes -- and real ugly teeth -- kept on truckin' or, as Texas/Southern country folks say, "It just boogied on down the road." Yeehaw - Gone!

A terrible and traumatic crisis was averted, which would have been a horrible memory no child should ever have to live with. Especially on top of everything else this little girl had been going through.

However, another "it" -- a monster storm called Harvey -- eventually floated down their street, turned its head, opened its jaws with its rows of sharp fangs, and devoured their home with tons of strong rainwater.

There was nothing this little girl's daddy could throw to stop this "alligator."

-- Event narrated by Rob Armstrong, 2017

Alligators were left homeless and wandering during the storm,
making a trek through the floodwaters dangerous.
Photo courtesy of C. Chapman

While alligators were seen in some flooded areas, other
creatures were trying to save their babies from the flood waters
too, such as this Mama Raccoon.
Photo courtesy of C. Chapman

XVI
Reaching Out to Help a Friend
by Ellen Lancaster

At 2:00 am on the first night of Harvey's "performance" when I couldn't sleep, I called my friend who lives on the bayou in Dickinson, just to check on her. She was nearly in hysterics when she answered the phone, telling me that she was upstairs in her underwear, looking out the window to figure how to get out of her home. She had waded through four-foot-deep water in her downstairs to get to the stairs so she could go up and out of the water.

She was 89 years old, and she kept repeating over and over again, "I just don't know what to do. I just don't know what to do."

I talked to her in the same kind of a voice I have used with kids and grandkids who were panicking about homework assignments or arguments with friends. I said, "You are going to go back downstairs and get whatever dry clothes you can find, bring them upstairs and put them on. Then you are going to call me back. While you are doing that, I will call the Dickinson Police and other emergency numbers. Don't think about anything else but clothes and getting back upstairs."

I called Dickinson P.D. and was told that there were boats on the bayou in her area and that they would go get her. That was a two-minute call. But the wait to hear back from my friend was a long ten minutes.

She did finally call, breathless, but successful. She was upstairs and dressed. As we talked, she suddenly shouted, "I'm up here! I'm up here in the window. See? I'm right here. Yes, I need a rescue!"

She told me the rest of this story after she finally made it to my house -- two days later. What I had heard on the phone was her calling out to a boat that was in her driveway, not in the bayou behind her house. A young man was able to get to her, carry her downstairs and load her into the boat, where there were already four other evacuees. She was the last person picked up in that load, and she never learned who her rescuers were. She did know that they were not the police, but rather volunteers.

By the time she was rescued, it was past 3:00 am. By 4:00 am, she and the others in her boat had been deposited onto the Gulf Freeway. Apparently, that had become the dumping station so the rescue boats could go back for more people in distress.

There she was -- a very elderly woman, alone in the night with nothing but her clothes. She didn't have even her cell phone, which she had dropped into the water in her living room while being carried out of her home.

Before she could start crying again, someone called her name! It was her yard maintenance man, who had been working all night to fish people out of their bayou homes. He became her knight in shining armor, taking her home with him, where she spent the next night. After a bath and a few hours' sleep, she called me from his home.

After I had heard the whole tale, I told her I would come to get her. Only then did I hear that there was no way to get from the other side of the freeway, where she was, to my home in League City, where we were high and dry. Between us and the freeway was high water and major flooding. It was late the next day before her "knight" was able to deliver her to our doorstep in his huge truck.

For the next month, she lived with us, while I, my husband, and our son -- and several other volunteers – worked to clean out her house, piling all her worldly goods onto the curb in front of her house.

My main memory of those days is of the smell carried within the inches-thick mud all through her downstairs rooms and the smell of the mold and rotten food in her refrigerator. That was accompanied by the terrifying feeling of sliding through mud on the tile floors, with only a push broom for balance.

This pile of debris in Laurel Field, Friendswood, is typical of the one described by Ellen Lancaster. These were seen along the edges of streets for weeks following the storm.
Photo courtesy of Patricia Vance

All of us in the work crew were ourselves rescued by a contractor who took over the job and actually did the work he promised to do, and in a timely fashion.

I wish I could say I look back at the month as a time in which our friendship flowered. The combination of being almost 90 years old, dealing with the loss of everything but her life and bank account, and having to start over in every way -- from toilet paper to lamps to beds to paintings to cars (plus not getting any support from her children) was too much for my friend.

She became more and more disoriented and angry toward whomever she had to deal with. Trying to plan how we could help her often became an argument, while she tried to remember words and focus on decisions. Sadly, I decided the project had grown too big for my husband and myself to manage, and we handed her over to her (very reluctant) children.

I am glad that we were able to help a friend in need. But I am sorry it ended in the loss of a friend. I learned that we all handle stress differently, depending on our emotional strength, our physical strength -- and our age. I'm sure there were many elderly people who experienced the same feelings of disorientation, frustration, and anger after Harvey.

Next time, I'll be better prepared.

XVII
Tied to Your Heart Forever
by Jackie May

We first met Todd and Katie in the summer of 2016 as we walked our dogs in the apartment complex where we all lived in Friendswood. As young newlyweds, they had recently moved into our building and lived in the upstairs apartment around the corner from our downstairs apartment. We soon discovered that we shared a common bond because we were all new in town.

Over the next year, they chatted with us as our dogs played or if we happened to see them at the mailroom during the day. We enjoyed our conversations with Todd and Katie, whether it was discussing our work, our neighborhood or our dogs.

In late August of 2017, we heard that a hurricane could possibly impact our area. Since we do not have any family that lives in this area and we had never experienced a hurricane before, we thought we should make a plan in case the storm became a threat to our home and family. On our walk that evening, we saw Todd and asked if we and our teenage daughter could come upstairs to their apartment if the storm became bad (never dreaming it would get *that* bad). He said of course we could, and we exchanged numbers.

When Hurricane Harvey hit our town, we were inundated with non-stop rain. As water began to rise in our home, we texted Todd and Katie, asking if we could come up to their place. They not only heartily agreed but also invited us to bring our dog. Todd made several trips down through the floodwaters to our apartment and helped my husband bring our most important items, including food and water, up to safety. (Miraculously, as the water outside covered the air conditioning units, we never lost power throughout the entire hurricane. God's hand of protection and provision, and His presence encircled us).

Over the course of several hours, Todd noticed that another neighbor and his family who lived in a downstairs apartment had nowhere to go to escape the rising water in their home. They were a family of five; a dad, mom, nine-year-old daughter, and twin babies. Todd asked them to come up to their apartment and to bring their pets.

Todd and Katie opened their home to all of us, welcoming us with a safe refuge from the floodwaters of our homes, offering a place to sleep, a warm shower, a place to wash our clothes -- and Todd even made dinner for us!

Eventually, as boats began to come to rescue anyone who wasn't able to make it to safety, Todd went through the floodwaters to offer bottles of water to the rescuers.

Days later, as the waters began to recede enough for us to go out to assess the damage to our home, Todd and Katie were right there with us. Even though they had suffered flood damage to their garage and its contents, they were willing to do anything they could to help us, both physically and emotionally.

After Todd helped us rip up all the wet, heavy carpet and set it at the curb, he set up dehumidifiers (that he already had) in our home to help remove the moisture. He and Katie helped us go through what we were able to salvage, pack it up and take it upstairs to their apartment since we had nowhere else to put it. After the waters receded enough that the roads were drivable, Todd drove us to the rental car location, to the store and anywhere else we needed to go.

After they helped us take our salvageable contents up to their apartment, Todd and Katie began checking on our other neighbors, making sure all were okay and helping them in any way they could. Katie filled up a cooler with ice, water, and cold drinks and left the cooler on their front porch, telling everyone in the neighborhood to help themselves to the refreshing drinks.

Many families struggled to clear out wet, soggy carpets, clothes, wallboard, etc. after flood waters receded. This was a common scene across the area as neighbor helped neighbor to recover.
Photo courtesy of Patricia Vance

As we (and our neighbors) were all working to make sense of the tragedy and how we would move forward, Todd and Katie went around to our immediate neighbors, asking what they would like to have to eat from a local BBQ place. Then, they both went and ordered the food, paid for it and brought it back to all of us. They wouldn't take any of our money. They were just there to help and be a blessing for our neighborhood.

We stayed with Todd and Katie in their home for two weeks, until we were able to find a new place to live. In all that time, we never once felt that we were a bother to them, and they told us we could stay as long as we needed.

This photo expresses the conflicting position of many families during Harvey. While water crept close to their own homes, they welcomed neighbors and friends in need.

Photo courtesy of Patricia Vance

After we moved out, Katie's parents and Todd made and delivered a headboard (which they brought to our new home) for our daughter. She had admired the headboard in the spare bedroom where we had stayed while we were at their house. They had taken notice of that and since our daughter had lost her bed in the hurricane, Todd, Katie, and her parents blessed our daughter with a beautiful replica of the headboard she had admired.

If Todd and Katie had not welcomed us with open arms, we can honestly say that we don't know what our family would have done or where we would have gone in order to ensure our safety during Hurricane Harvey.

So much about a person's true character is shown in the midst of a crisis. Todd and Katie showed us maturity, love, and compassion far beyond their years. Their character and reflection of "Christ in Action" is something that my husband and I can only hope to live up to.

In looking back to that summer of 2016 when we "happened" to meet our new neighbors on a casual walk with our dog, we never dreamed that two years later, we would consider Todd and Katie as much a part of our family as our immediate family.

You never know…. Someone you casually meet could someday be tied to your heart forever.

XVIII

The Year of Harvey the Horrible:
Through the Eyes of a Gulf Coast Gal
By Carolyn Ferrell Watts

Flames fill the sky. Smoke irritates my eyes and breathing is difficult. I'd left the shelter to check on a victim who'd been standing in the parking lot for an hour, staring at the flames she had just escaped from. Her fiancé had been following her car, but his truck hadn't made it out of the blazing forest surrounding their farm. Smoke can stop a vehicle's motor. I stand with her until she can accompany me into the shelter.

On September 4, 2011, sparks from wind-damaged power lines fell onto drought-damaged grass and leaves near Bastrop State Park and started wildfires. By the 11th of that month, the fires had caused four deaths and destroyed 1700 homes.[1]

I was one of many mental health professionals who organized to help meet the various needs of the area communities during that disaster. My assignment was to assist in establishing and managing Smithville's shelter for fire victims and to counsel as needed.

The stories and emotions of volunteer firefighters who'd watched their own homes, farms and ranches burn as they fought to save the houses of others touched my heart. But this woman's agony as hope for her husband dwindled was heartbreaking.

Our debriefing process after the disaster helped me decide to agree with my husband's recent request that we move back to

---

[1]Wikipedia

Houston and reside closer to his daughter. An aggressive form of multiple sclerosis had deteriorated her health until she was existing in a paraplegic state, and she needed our help.

I shared my decision with him. "Honey, I don't feel safe here anymore. The fire was just blocks from our home! Had sparks blown across the Colorado River, the 100-year-old homes in our neighborhood would have been doomed. I'm a Gulf Coast gal and know what to do during a hurricane. When a storm enters the Gulf of Mexico, there is usually at least a week's notice, enabling people to prepare for it or get the hey away! There are also advance warnings of tornados such as those that destroyed your sister's home. But wildfires can occur without any notice. I'm ready to move. I want a house that is surrounded by water!"

Our house sold the day after we listed it with a realtor, and we had one month to find another and move. We chose a house in League City that met my specifications of preparedness for -- and safety from -- storms:

- It had survived Hurricane Ike.
- It had a gas stove and fireplace that could function during power outages.
- The pleasant, man-made lake behind the house was designed to serve as a detention pond to prevent flooding.

My husband teased, "Can you be happy with water behind the house rather than surrounding it?"

I've always taken hurricanes seriously because storms have affected several of my family members. Sitha Burton Ferrell, brother of my paternal great-great-great grandfather Jabez Ferrell (1789-1866) and his bride Adeline drowned during their honeymoon in 1874 when a storm off the coast of Galveston sank the wooden ship they were in.

One month after my birth in Beaumont, Texas, a hurricane hit our area near Galveston County causing 19 deaths and injuring hundreds. There were no weather satellites at the time and ship reports of storm conditions were silenced to prevent detection by a World War II enemy submarine. So advance warning was almost non-existent.

From 1943 until Hurricane Harvey in 2017, the southeast Texas Gulf Coast experienced approximately 47 hurricanes.[2] Hurricane Audrey made landfall near the Texas/Louisiana border on June 27, 1957. In Cameron, Louisiana, the only structure that survived was the courthouse. A year later, I accompanied my grandmother when she visited a friend in Cameron whose family had been impacted. My awareness of the dangers of hurricanes increased while hearing how (before their rescue via boat) the family had put their baby on a top kitchen cabinet shelf to keep her safe as winds buffeted their home and surges of water entered the house. Their fears were intensified by snakes and alligators that were also struggling to find anything they could crawl upon to escape the flood.

On September 14, 2008, Hurricane Ike destroyed the Bolivar beach house belonging to two cousins, Cheryl and Kay.

And unfortunately, in 2017, Hurricane Harvey destroyed Cheryl's Lake Charles home, so she now lives in the rebuilt beach house, hoping 2022 will be the year her home is repaired and livable.

Our new home in League City served us well when "Harvey the Horrible" arrived -- and stayed -- in 2017. Harvey destroyed 16,930 homes and damaged 290,063 homes. At least 68 deaths are directly attributed to Harvey's forces, making it the deadliest

[2]www: weather.gov/Houston/Galveston TX

hurricane in Texas since 1919. An additional 35 deaths are indirectly attributed to Harvey. NOAA estimates a $125 billion damage toll for Harvey, making it the second costliest hurricane in U.S. history (when adjusting for inflation) and the costliest hurricane in Texas history.[3]

The only damage I sustained from the flooding was a painful, swollen knee that occurred when I fell during our 2:00 am evacuation to the two-story home of kind neighbors.

Fortunately, the flood waters receded before they reached our front porch.

At the height of Harvey's onslaught, many people looked outside their homes such as in this neighborhood in Friendswood to find the storm lapping at their front steps.
Photo courtesy of Gary Macdonell

---

[3]https://en.wikipedia.org/wiki/List_of_Texas_hurricanes_(1980-present)

The noise from the whirling blades of rescue helicopters overhead reminded me of scenes from the MASH series or newscasts concerning various military conflicts during my life. It also triggered memories of similar sounds at military bases we visited to see our sons before their deployment.

During and after Harvey, I was awed by the goodness of people everywhere helping one another. The volunteers were amazing! The Turnley Family story (also in this book) illustrates how victims were helped in many ways.

The arrival of the Cajun Navy from Louisiana was of tremendous assistance. Members of our church, including some who were 80 or 90 years of age, participated in transporting, feeding, hauling materials, and cleaning for families whose homes were damaged by flood water from four inches to eight feet deep. They served in shelters and other areas. For months, our church shared space with various denominations that had lost their facilities to flood waters or that needed space to assist victims.

Over a year after Harvey's "visit," I was still counseling victims whose homes were damaged or destroyed. Timely repairs were delayed due to the vast number of places in need. Costs for materials had risen, and monies from FEMA were no longer adequate for repairing or rebuilding.

However, it is reassuring that town and city leaders learned lessons from the Harvey experience that they are now developing into actions that will limit future tragedies from hurricanes such as this.

Perhaps even more promising were my observations during the storm of the innate spirit of human caring and goodness that was evident everywhere!

XIX

Together in Spirit and Courage:
The Turnley Family Faces Harvey
By Carolyn Ferrell Watts

Brad Turnley and two of his sons, Cazzel (15) and Caden (17), struggled against the power of forceful winds as they waded through cold, dirty, knee-deep water toward their home across the street. Cold, stinging mist felt like tiny needles pricking their faces. The sky beneath a canopy of impenetrable dark clouds was peppered with lightning.

The trio had been watching the televised Mayweather vs. McGregor fight since 11:00 pm at a neighbor's home. They perceived their home to be a safe haven from storms as it had survived other Gulf Coast hurricanes without flooding.

The Turnleys' three-level home is on a hill that elevates their front yard approximately four feet above street level. The back yard is eight feet above street level and 20 feet from Geisler Bayou, a tributary of Dickinson Bayou.

By midnight, when the Turnley guys left for their home, the water was three feet high and rising in the street; torrential rains hammered the two brothers and their dad. Caden's peripheral vision detected his mother Tascha and little brother Dane (11) on their porch.

As her oldest son approached them, Tascha urged him to move everything out of his bedroom, which took up the entire first floor. Caden responded, "I will move my things onto my bed, but just to make you stop worrying, Mom. My room will be fine."

The Turnley Family Home
as it appeared before Hurricane Harvey
Photo courtesy of the Turnley Family

Tom Sawyer and Huck Finn would have enjoyed the young family's lifestyle in their home on the edge of Geisler Bayou. The fertile land is home to large trees that inspired the building of tree houses for the kids in previous years. A family dock extended over the dark green water of the bayou behind the house and was perfect for fishing or diving. The dock also enabled easy access into the family's kayaks, canoe and/or rowboat. These were usually parked next to the 21-foot boat that was often used for fishing or pleasure-riding in nearby Galveston Bay or Gulf of Mexico.

The boys frequently used the smaller vessels to visit their grandparents who lived one mile away by road or just a single city block away by water. Upon arriving for such visits, the youths would phone or text their parents to reassure them of their safe arrival, in compliance with family rules.

However, on August 27, 2017, the family fleet served in the vital rescue missions of over 100 people.

The Turnley family quickly realized that the improbable was going to happen in the coming storm: The flood waters had already overrun the banks of the bayou and invaded the yard, rising high enough to endanger their home.

Cazzel and Brad waded through the dark, churning bayou waters to unhitch their boat from its trailer which had been parked in the back yard. Caden hurried to his room and discovered that water was already seeping under his bedroom door and oozing up through cracks in the floor.

As Caden finished moving his valuables on to his bed, he noticed his walls were becoming damp. A couple of seconds later, the plaster began peeling off as water rushed through, pouring into his room. Stairs to the second floor started swelling until they could not absorb any more water and released suddenly, contributing to his growing concern that his room was no longer safe. The teenager acknowledged the reality that his possessions were about to be destroyed and took action, shouting to his family, "I need y'all to help NOW!"

Scrambling for his things and taking as much as possible on each trip, Caden moved all that he could carry and placed it on the living room floor, located on the second story. The entire family pitched in, trying to remove everything from the room that they could, including the brothers' pet reptiles (boas and corn snakes). They put everything into the living room where all the electronics and other valuable thngs had already been moved.

Breathing heavily and drenched in sweat, Caden turned to his dad and asked, "Is it going to stop raining anytime soon?"

The tall, slender, 17-year-old already knew the answer. But Caden's hopeful optimism lasted only a split second until the older male responded, "I don't think so."

Over the course of the next couple of hours, Caden noticed that the floor in the living room went from a smooth light brown wood to discolored dark brown with a rough, uneven texture, especially between the planks. The floor looked like a topographic map because of the water swelling. It was frightening to realize that everything he had saved from his room had been placed in an area that could still be affected if the water continued rising into the main part of the house on the second floor.

Caden knew that his brother's bedroom on the third floor would be safe from water damage. He begged, "Cazzel, can you please help me move my things to your room?" He couldn't tell if the younger boy's skin was pale from exhaustion or shock when he responded, "Sure."

They began by getting on both sides of a large speaker and hoisting it up. The brothers grunted and struggled with every step from extreme fatigue. For about ten minutes they painstakingly moved anything they could, transferring clothes, boxes, photo albums and electronics upstairs.

In the midst of the chaos from moving things upstairs and uncertain about what to do next, Cazzel said, "Why don't we pray?" The family stopped, held hands and led by Brad, prayed, *"God use us to help others and keep us safe."*

The family's television had stopped working, so they didn't know how extensive the flooding was. Cazzel later stated, "We thought it was only our street that was flooding and had no idea it would flood into Dickinson and Houston."

As they were viewing the alarming sight of rising waters from a window, an older neighbor called them; she was very scared. They offered to pick her up in their boat and bring her to their house because it was higher. She responded that she wanted to stay in her home and ride it out but thanked them for the offer.

The flooded street as seen through the front window
of the Turnley house during Hurricane Harvey
Photo courtesy of the Turnley Family

The entire family was on constant watch to see how high the water was rising. They decided that their neighbor was probably going to be safe but assured her that if she began to feel unsafe, she should call them and they would pick her up in their boat.

At about five in the morning, after hours of moving things around and worrying about how high the water would get, Caden stumbled upstairs into his brother's closet because it was isolated. He was wondering how bad the storm had actually been outside of their neighborhood, and if the water would continue to rise. With his stomach burning from hunger, eyes aching and losing focus from extreme exhaustion, he'd had enough!

At that point, he began to tell himself that everything would be alright. While repeating this over and over in his head, Caden slowly drifted into sleep, curled up on the floor in the closet. Using a towel for a pillow, he slept for about three hours, waking at 8:00 am.

Cazzel finally went to sleep at about 5:30 am with his 11-year-old brother, but he was unable to sleep more than a couple of hours. When he awoke, he was shocked to see three inches of water in their living room, and it was still raining. Sleep would not return to him, and he worried when the flooding would stop.

His parents had stayed up through the night to keep watch on the water level. All members of the family were aware of the constant heavy rains barraging their home, and their nerves were on edge.

Cazzel and his dad left the house early and swam through about eight feet of very cold, dirty, constantly surging bayou and sewer water to reach their fishing boat which had floated off its trailer in the backyard. He and his dad picked up neighbors in the boat, including the elderly lady who had called earlier, and eight people who had been staying at the neighbor's house across the street.

According to Cazzel, he and his dad were really in shock. It felt like a dream that Dickinson was under water and that they were driving their boat on the streets. It didn't seem real or even possible.

The Turnley men help evacuate neighbors
by boat during Hurricane Harvey
Photo courtesy of the Turnley Family

When neighbors saw them coming in the boat, they were really happy to be rescued, but also sad. Many were leaving behind cars and houses that were being destroyed. One rescue included a family with two children (a boy, 5, and a girl, about 7), their parents, friends, a cat and a dog. The pets were freaking out: They seemed to want to jump out of the boat, but not into the water. They looked frantic.

By 7:30 am, the rain had subsided, but sporadic showers continued. Cazzel and Brad could hear fan-boats or airboats, but there were no other boats on their street. Residents of ground-level houses had fled to rooftops. Sounds of helicopter blades churning overhead reminded them of movies and news stories of military conflicts. A Coast Guard helicopter was evacuating flood victims into lowered cages.

Caden reported that when he woke up, he walked downstairs and saw water in the house. His family's two kayaks with their oars inside were floating down the street. His dad and Cazzel had left in the fishing boat. Feeling very tired and not really thinking, just reacting, Caden swam a short distance (perhaps 20 feet) to the largest kayak, pulled himself onto it and began to paddle down their street onto Sunset Street.

A man with his family spied Caden and asked if he would paddle him to his truck so that he could retrieve a plastic bag of their clothes. Caden obliged the man, then returned him to his family. They were then able to wade in the knee-deep water to a higher area a couple of streets down. The two adults and children (perhaps 8 years of age) thanked him. Caden sadly apologized because they could salvage only the bag of clothes from their truck.

One of the Turnley men in a kayak assisting as others
of his family evacuate their neighbors by boat
Photo courtesy of the Turnley Family

As Caden paddled back toward his home, he noticed a woman walking in the water and floating a cooler next to her. He paddled over to her and learned that she lived on a hill that was safe, but she was worried about her elderly parents who were in the flooded area. They were all from South Africa.

He helped the family load things that they could save (photos and other valuables) into the cooler. They had put other items into their own floating coolers. It took Caden three trips to help the family and their small dog relocate to their daughter's house with their belongings. Caden remarked that they were surprisingly calm throughout the process.

By this time, Caden had joined his brother and their dad in searching for others who needed help. They had seven life jackets for them and four other people.

They passed one house that had a tree covering it, prohibiting a sky rescue. But there was a family of four on the roof, including a baby girl (perhaps a year old) and a toddler (about three). Because the Turnleys were in the boat, they approached in an effort to rescue the family. The children's chocolate lab had been unable to climb onto the roof and was swimming around the porch area. The water level was about three feet below the roof.

The family was very happy to see the Turnley men. Brad climbed a ladder that the residents had put up before the water had risen so high. Cazzel stood on the roof of a car near the ladder and his dad handed the baby to him. A low-flying helicopter stirred the water, knocking Cazzel's feet out from under him. He slipped off the car top but held the crying baby up above his head, managing to hand her safely to his brother on the boat.

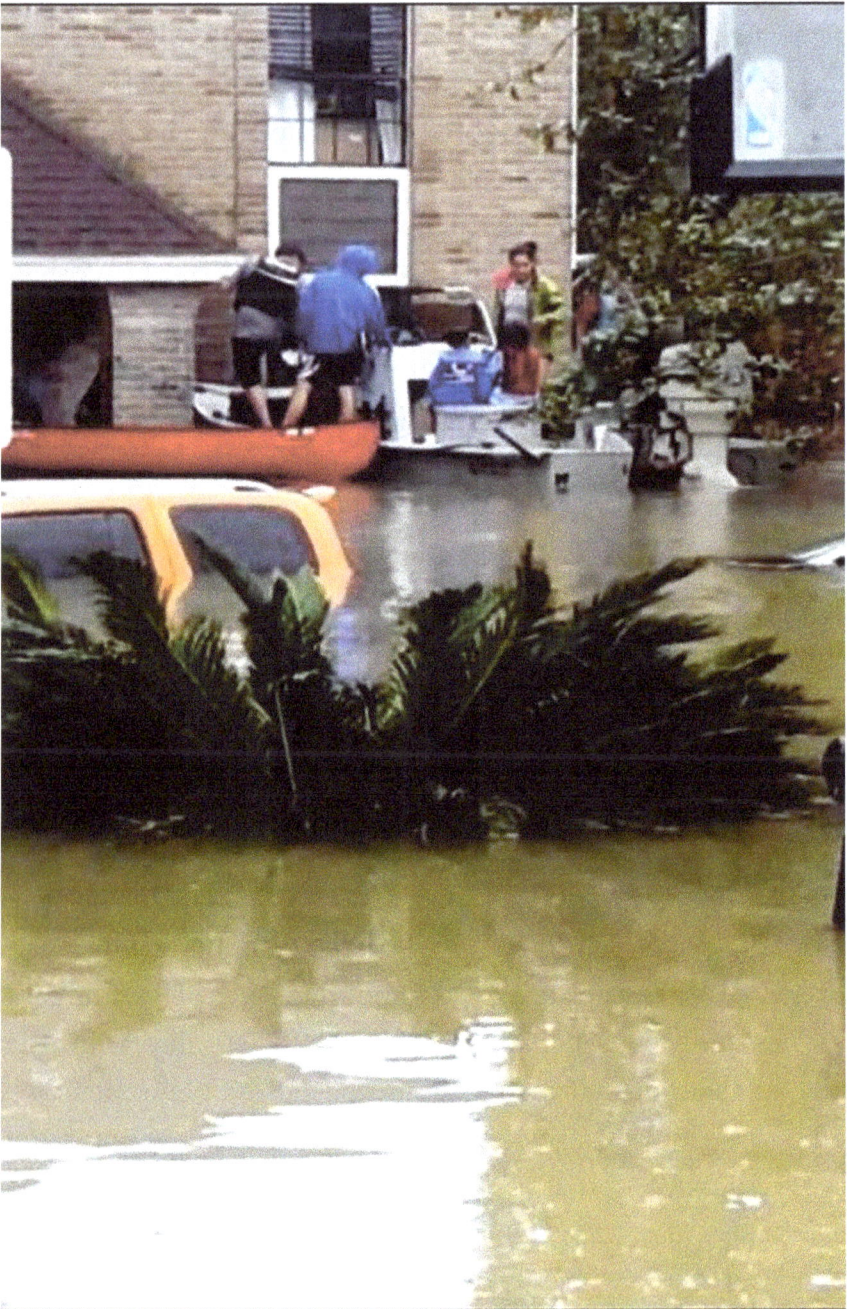

The Turnley men help a family stranded on their roof
during Hurricane Harvey
Photo courtesy of the Turnley Family

Shortly after this rescue, a woman waved to the three men in the fishing boat, signaling for help. Brad and Cazzel helped a father, daughter, a son and his wife onto the boat, then carried them to a safe area on FM 646. The older man was calm and collected, but his family was quiet, and one lady appeared to be in shock.

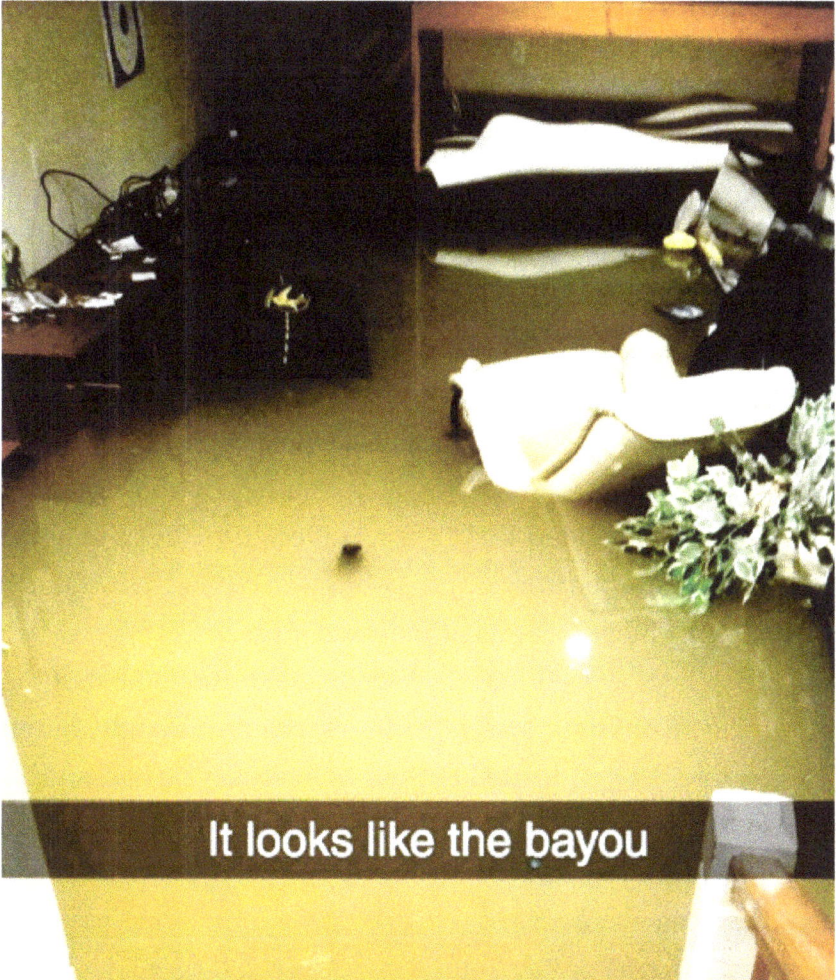

It looks like the bayou

Some of the destruction is reflected in this picture of Caden's first-floor bedroom after Harvey's unwelcome visit.
Photo courtesy of the Turnley Family

On another trip, the Turnleys helped evacuate a gentleman and his wife, and the man seemed familiar to Cazzel. Later, during a news reporter's interview, he learned that the male passenger had been Gene Krantz, who told the reporter that he was grateful to the family that had picked them up. Gene Kranz served as NASA's second Chief Flight Director, directing missions of the Gemini and Apollo programs, including the first lunar landing, Apollo 11. Kranz also helped Apollo 13's crew safely return to earth after a life-threatening situation developed in space. He is the author of *Failure is Not an Option*. Cazzel explained that Krantz was the guy who wore a white vest in the movie *Apollo 13*. Caden recalled that Kranz had spoken at his school in 2017, when they had watched the movie and talked a lot about him.

When the brothers were asked if they had lost anything in the flood, Cassel responded that the waters destroyed Caden's bedroom, their living room, two cars, and their garage and all it contained. Caden stated that he had saved his television and X-Box but lost his bedframe and books. Cazzel added, "But he didn't lose his life; that is what we are happy about today."

The brothers agreed that they were able to save most of their things. They lost lawnmowers and cars, but nothing meaningful -- like people. They returned to their home a day or two after the flood to take some things to their grandmother's house. The water level had receded but was still in the street and in their house. But they were able to retrieve clothes and other items they had saved, such as guitars, etc.

They explained that two months prior to this conversation, their grandmother had moved to League City. Her previous home, located near theirs in Colonial Estates, was now destroyed in the flood. Had she not moved to the new location, they might not have had a place to stay. "We went to her house about five that afternoon and stayed until December 8, 2017."

The two Turnley boys in knee-deep floodwater
in front of their house
Photo courtesy of the Turnley Family

According to Caden and Cazzel, their house was not livable. One week after the flood, part of their house was now empty, and many friends and family members arrived to help clean out the rest of it. Their yard was still a mess and full of debris (now including plaster, nails, and wooden planks). The family also helped clean out the home of a lady down the street and that of the mother of a former teacher of the boys.

They estimated that by December 2018, their home had been completely repaired.

The Turnley brothers were asked to express their thoughts about how the experience affected them and to provide encouragement for others. Cazzel responded, "I think it positively impacted me. I know it had a negative impact on many. However, I feel like I now know what I can do when it comes down to a life-or-death situation. I am glad I had the experiences of helping others and watching Dickinson come together. It was a humbling experience."

He stated that he would encourage others by reassuring them that, "Everything happens for a reason, and life gets better. If there was a lesson to be learned, it is probably, to 'always keep a boat with you when you live in an area that can flood.'"

Cazzel and Caden Turnley standing outside
their home after Hurricane Harvey
Photo courtesy of the Turnley Family

Caden shared, "I don't think I will ever forget this event. It came out of nowhere. We could never have predicted a flood like this. Dickinson flooded in 1979, but not like this. A lot of people did leave Dickinson after this flood. One of my friends moved to higher ground in Clear Lake. However, all of Dickinson seemed very united and empathetic with others. People were walking around, giving out water and other items. People were helping one another with repairs, food, and clothing supplies. When we returned to school, everyone was glad to see that others were okay."

Postscript: The above experiences were taken from an interview that the author, Carolyn Watts, had with Cazzel and Caden Turnley, as well as from a paper that Caden wrote for his English II class on 10/13/2017.

In conversations with the brothers' grandmother, Sharon Turnley, the author learned that the two boys were out helping others for days after the storm. Their mother, Tascha, was also quite involved and encouraged others to help with the rescues.

Many Gulf Coast residents are hardy people who have coped with and survived multiple hurricanes during their lives. Repeated exposure to storms -- along with confidence in surviving them -- can desensitize people to the danger of a storm. In this case, residents were aware that the eye of the hurricane (the worst part) would not hit them.

So it was not surprising to hear that, when Tascha entered one area business just as the flooding began, the customers were casually sitting around, sipping beverages, and watching television accounts of the disaster. She reminded them that many others needed their help because Harvey was unique since it was flooding at a rate rarely seen during this lifetime. She roused additional volunteers, who realized their role in this storm was more important than is required by most storms.

And like the rest of Galveston, Harris, and the surrounding counties, all answered the call.

XX
To the Roof!
by Alyssa & Matt Baker

My husband Matt and I tucked our nine-year-old niece Lola and her dog into bed, and we took our dog Frank to our room. We all went to sleep easily the night before Hurricane Harvey hit, and I woke around 3:00 am to the sound of running water. I started to get up out of bed and stood in about six inches of water.

I woke Matt up, and he checked outside to see if he could drive us out of the neighborhood, but he saw that the water level in the street was covering our mailbox.

We were stuck. We called 9-1-1 and got busy signals all morning, so we called Matt's dad to give us some direction. I was seven months pregnant, and we had just had a baby shower, so I was trying to move all the gifts from the floor in the nursery to tables, shelves and beds – any higher surface!

We all quickly packed bags and sat at the highest point of our home -- our bed. Matt, I, Lola and our two dogs watched the water rise to the top of our mattress, and then the highest point in our home became the attic.

We took our bags, snacks and an axe and hoisted everyone into the attic to wait to be rescued. My husband waded back through the water outside to try to flag down boats. I was taking phone calls from family and friends, some of whom were trying to rescue us, and others who were trying to figure out how they could help. We watched the water rise and prayed for the rain to stop. And I took deep breaths in fear that I might go into labor from the stress of the morning's events.

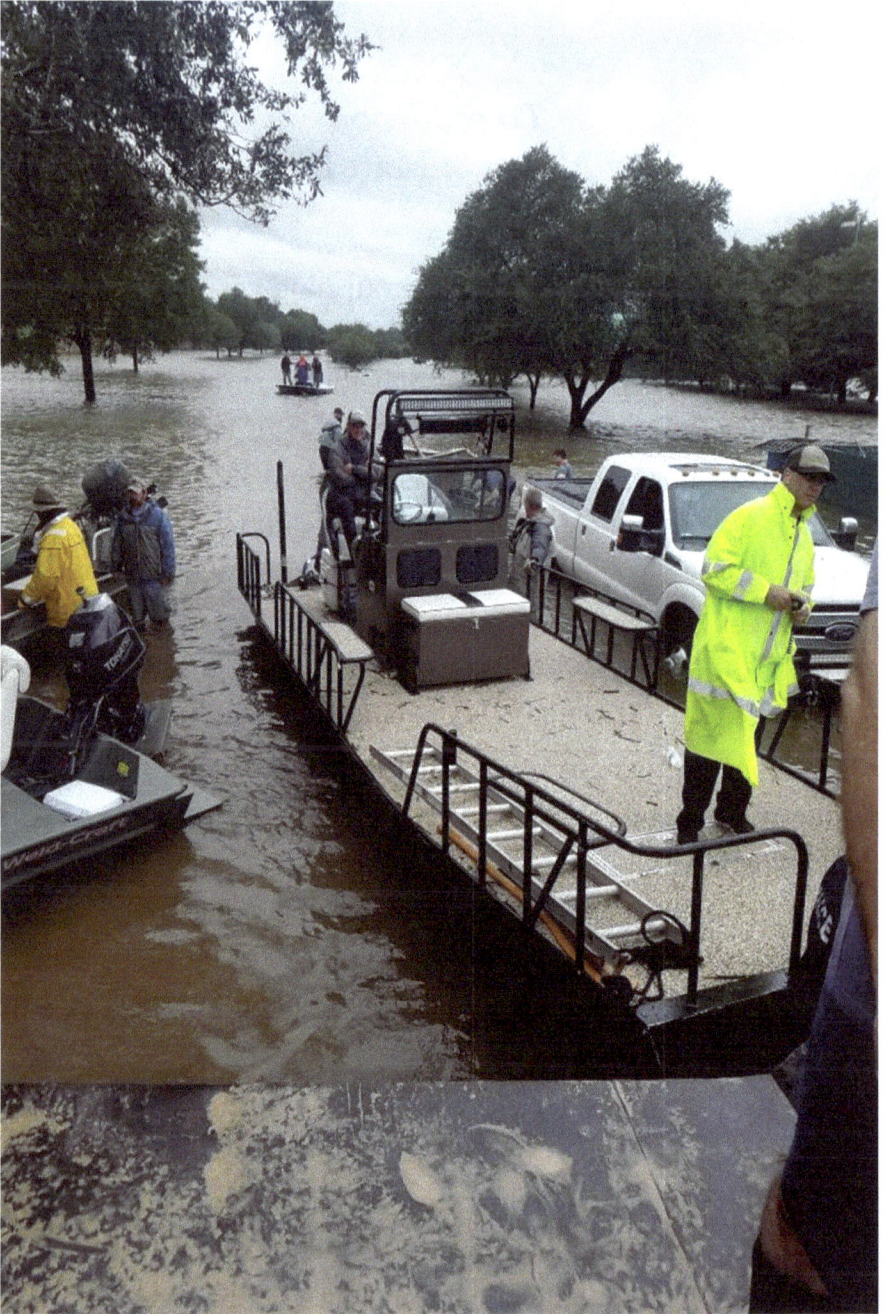

Rescues such as described by the Bakers took place in trucks,
boats, kayaks -- and by wading through swirling waters.
Photo courtesy of Gary Macdonell

Matt and I had been involved in a couples' small group with our church for about a year at that time, and we had a Houston police officer and a Galveston County judge from our group talking with us, letting us know that the Coast Guard would come and get us in a helicopter. To do that, we needed to get onto our roof. The only way to get dogs, a nine-year-old child, and a very pregnant lady up on the roof would be through the attic.

So my husband began swinging and chopping through the roof with an axe. He was able to break through and make a hole big enough for all of us to get out.

We saw helicopters and many boats come and go with the promise to come back for us. After seven hours of sitting in the attic, we were rescued by a neighbor in a boat. He pulled into our driveway, and we all climbed down the roof -- with only about a one-foot drop from the roof to the boat. We then were taken to a church in our neighborhood and from there were transported by the National Guard toward Texas City. We were stopped on the access road to I-45 for a while and were picked up by my sister-in-law's father, who lives in Galveston. He took all of us back to their home where we got showers, called loved ones, cried quite a bit, and ate gumbo—a lot of gumbo!

Our families drove to be with us as soon as the roads opened. My dad brought family friends with him and supplies to begin gutting our home and saving what we could. We lived in my dad's beach house in Galveston until we were able to move back into our home in time for Thanksgiving.

With the help of Clear Creek Community Church, family, friends, Matt's student athletes and their families, co-workers, and many others in our community, we were able to repair and move back into our home after only 87 days of construction.

Trash piles like this were a common sight for weeks after
the storm as families "mucked out" their homes and
began the rebuilding process.
Photo courtesy of Gary Macdonell

We were able to get ready for our son to be born, get our niece
back to school, and get ourselves back to a somewhat normal
routine within a very short amount of time. We were so grateful
for all the monetary support, emotional support -- and physical
labor.

We know that without those whom God has placed into our
lives, we would not have made it out of this event whole. We
consider ourselves blessed and beyond grateful.

XXI

Dramatic/Traumatic Rescues:
Compliments of Hurricane Harvey
by **Chris and Christopher Barden**
(as told to Patricia Vance)

August 26-27, 2017

The first rain band of the storm struck Friendswood in the early morning on Saturday, August 26, 2017. It waned by afternoon and water even receded in the front yard. That was deceptive: Extremely heavy rains and flooding started late Saturday night and continued into early Sunday morning.

Our extended family had four houses flooded in this quaint small town. This included:

- Parents Chris and Marti Barden (two inches of water)
- Son Christopher Barden (18 inches)
- Daughter Ashley Armstrong (18 inches)
- And a business office in a house (10 inches)

Chris' and Christopher's homes were about a half mile apart and family members could still travel this section of the connecting road FM 518. Ashley lived across the out-of-its-banks and forceful Clear Creek and could not be reached because of deep-water flooding at the bridge on FM 528.

Ashley's house was the most critical because of its location but also because she and her husband Rob and their young daughter Brianah are Little People/Dwarfs. They also have a younger son Mason and two Lab dogs. And Ashley was three to four months pregnant.

When water of one to two inches deep began to invade

Ashley's home, she kept watch with the children at the front door, hoping to flag down a rescue truck for help. They wanted to leave ASAP, not knowing how high the water would get.

The water had reached four to five inches deep when a big dump truck saw the children and stopped to load them all, including the dogs. Since the water was already getting too deep in the front yard for them to walk, Ashley, Rob, and the kids were carried to the truck.

After also picking up some of their neighbors, the truck drove them all to a central location. The nearest one was a church on high ground by the creek.

A quick note (from the author) about this church and its parishioners: These folks did not know their building would be a sudden makeshift shelter for those forced out of their wet homes. The pastor, out of the goodness of his heart, opened the church and said, in effect, "Welcome, please come in." These flood victims had nowhere else to go and here they found "room at the inn." However, the church was not set up to house and feed about 100 people and pets on a moment's notice. They did the best they could with what was on hand, which consisted of some cheese crackers and goldfish-shaped crackers for the children. Not enough food for everyone, but they were blessed with enough bottled water.

No one had expected a flood, much less this much high water. It was not intended to happen, and all affected were shocked and caught off guard.

Since Rob and Ashley had the two dogs, they were directed to the fellowship hall for people with pets. There were no pillows, blankets, cots or carpet so they went to sleep on a concrete floor. About 2:00 am on August 27, someone managed to get through and deliver a few blankets. These were used as pillows.

All that day, August 27, various friends and relatives tried to get to the church to rescue Ashley and her family but, by then, the building was encircled with too much high water. The homeless inside remained confined in this haven.

August 28, 2017

The intense rain eased up early the following morning and there seemed to be a lull in the storm. Chris and Marti's house was water free. Christopher and his family were brought over from their flooded house. His sister Amy's house was not flooded, but she was at her parents' home for reassurance and togetherness.

All of Chris and Marti's furniture that had been raised on bricks was lowered to the now-dry floor. A big breakfast was cooked for the crowd.

They agreed that, certainly, the worst of the storm was over, and they all could breathe a sigh of relief. However, the biggest worry remained: Ashley and her family were missing, still stuck in the church's instant shelter.

Suddenly, time was of the essence as word came that the helicopters and boats were moving in to air lift the church refugees to Dallas at 2:00 pm. Ashley had to get out and away now! Big D was not an option. Besides, her Dad had promised her donuts when he got her to his house.

A daring plot was launched, with a decisive plan devised by Ashley's father and brother. The rain started again around 10:30 am as they headed off across the bridge. The plan....

Phase One: Chris packed up his two dogs, left his home and crossed the drenched yard to a neighbor's flooded house to

borrow his kayak. (The neighbor was in Europe and couldn't get home, so he missed the whole show.)

However, rather than depending on a kayak, another neighbor had an SUV and offered to take Chris to find a passable route to the Clear Creek bridge on FM 528 (the unofficial west side of NASA Road One.) Many routes and out-of-the-way detours had to be discovered and tried before they finally got to the desired location, as the direct route on FM 518 toward FM 528 was flooded too high to cross the bridge on Coward's Creek.

The City of Friendswood is on the west side of the bridge on FM 528 and the City of Webster is on the east side. The church is a quarter mile further east on the same road. After finding the "Northwest Passage" detour, Chris and his neighbor drove back to Chris' house to get the kayak, Christopher, and his sisters Leah and Amy.

Another quick note (from the author): What a difference higher elevation makes, even on the same road. So many of the main roads were flooded with up to five feet of water. The power of flood water is nothing to mess around with. Even when it looks still and "not too deep," it's usually deceptive. This kind of H_2O demands respect.

Christopher had called his good friend Johnny Franklin, a former Marine with a pickup truck, to help if he could get out. Fortunately, Johnny's house had escaped the wrath of several creeks that were ganging up on the city. Living on the Webster/east side of the bridge, he was able to take back roads (and several median dividers) to get to the church.

Leah and Amy, Chris and Christopher took the same long detour route as Chris had found earlier, but now they were in the neighbor's SUV with the kayak on the roof.

They drove as close as possible to the west side of the bridge before the road became impassable and were able to get about a quarter mile away from it. The vehicle was carrying grandmother's wheelchair for Ashley's husband Rob and all the portable/nonperishable food from Marti's pantry and refrigerator to share with others still hunkered down in the church.

They parked the SUV at what would be the pick-up point for Ashley and her family. From there, they would drive back to their parents' home and safety, where everyone else was prayerfully waiting.

Phase Two: Chris and Christopher unloaded the kayak from the SUV and loaded the cargo into the kayak. Surveying the landscape, the pair saw several stalled-out cars, with water climbing up the tires as it began to rain again. The top of the bridge was dry, but both ends of the bridge were over waist deep in water. (Dry in this case means not under flood water, but still wet from rain).

With Leah and Amy staying safe in the SUV, it was time for some heavy "he-man" work to begin. Chris and Christopher pulled the fully loaded kayak by rope to the edge of the bridge where the water was about 3.5 feet deep with a strong current. The far side of the bridge also had the same level of rushing creek water where it met the road.

Finally, up and over the bridge and down the other side. They still had another quarter mile walk through shallow, overflowed creek water while towing the packed kayak. They had to get as close as possible to the place where Johnny was waiting with the family without endangering his truck.

Chris Barden and his son Christopher help to rescue their
daughter/sister and her family from FM 528 in Friendswood
(with a kayak and wheelchair)
Photo courtesy of Leah Barden

Thank goodness for strong men! Chris and Christopher must have eaten their Wheaties for breakfast! (Just kidding! In truth, both are Supermen.)

But now there was a new problem! Rob could not swim and, even with a life jacket, he could not ride in the kayak. If it tipped in the swift-flowing, waist-deep water, he would be gone. Oh God, what to do?

When Chris and Christopher got to shallower water on the east side of the bridge, they saw two men (strangers) who were trying to work up the courage to walk their small, flat-bottom aluminum boat across the rushing water. Their boat battery had died, and their friend had left the boat for them to retrieve.

One asked if Chris and Christopher could help them get their boat over the bridge to the west side. The men said they had watched the father-and-son rescue team come through the four-foot, fast-flowing current and they were impressed.

At this point, the tiny fishing boat looked like a huge luxury yacht to Chris, so he yelled back, "Have I got a deal for you! You see that pickup truck over there? It has a family of Little People in it who are waiting for us, and I need you to help me get them across the bridge (east to west). And I will help you get your boat across the bridge."

The men agreed with a verbal handshake and joined the rescue mission. When Chris got to Johnny's truck, Rob said that, as he had watched them pulling the kayak through the deeper flood waters, he thought maybe staying at the church really wasn't that bad after all.

Phase Three: The two young children were loaded into the kayak. Rob and Ashley, along with dogs and suitcases, were helped into the boat. All wore life jackets. The four men walked and pulled this wagon train back through the waist-deep, fast-moving current of water at the base of the bridge.

Arriving at the bridge, the passengers were unloaded to walk across the dry portion at the top of bridge. Rob rode in the wheelchair, pushed by his father-in-law, while the children walked. Ashley walked across the bridge escorted on her dad's arm: What a woman! Such a wonderful loving father and brother who risked their own safety with brave hearts to save those they loved!

As Rob was watching the rest of the family from a safe distance, a policeman friend of his pulled up in an old Army truck and asked if he was by himself. After conversing with Rob for a minute, the policeman drove off. (See the end of this story for a follow-up to this brief interaction.)

A water rescue in Friendswood
Photo courtesy of Gary Macdonell

Now the four men got the boats that had been patiently waiting on the dry concrete area and walked them over the top of the bridge to where the high water started again on the west side.

Johnny went home after his rescued passengers Ashley and family were picked up by the Bardens at the designated rendezvous point. He had to immediately go check on his own family and house to make sure nothing had occurred while he was gone. Water had been almost to the front porch step when he left to help out his Barden friends.

Everyone resumed their previous seats for the last leg of the cruise, and the fight with the flood water began again. Victory was secured by muscle and brute force. Maybe an unseen Angel helped, too.

This complete trek, from the church pick-up area to the SUV's waiting area and over the bridge was several hundred yards long. With multiple trips, that was a lot of wading and hauling.

Phase Four: Eventually, everyone and everything were loaded into the designated vehicles and ready to be driven away from this "mean ole nasty floodwater."

After fulfilling the bargain with the two strangers to deliver their small boat to the Friendswood side, Chris and the entire family expressed intense relief, sincere thanks, and genuine goodbyes to the rescue guys with their mercy ship.

What a job of strength and endurance: The team worked, and God provided. Faith and action make for a great and successful partnership! Glory to God. He answered lots of prayers, and praise and thanks were given to Him.

Phase Five: Mission accomplished! All were brought home at last to the waiting arms of a mother's love.

There was a very tearful, emotional family reunion at Chris and Marti's home. The family was together and had survived the horrible flood from Hurricane Harvey. It was a full house with nine adults, six children and five dogs. Unfortunately, there was no place open or accessible to buy donuts for Ashley, as promised. Yet, after all -- in spite of it all -- it turned out to be a happy day because the family was united, safe and secure.

Towards evening, the rains started to get heavier and heavier.

Before bedtime, the family formed a circle, held hands, and said a prayer for more safety and mercy.

The family leaders knew that the house would take on water, so they took as much stuff upstairs as they could and raised the remaining furniture on bricks.

August 29, 2017

The second band of heavy rain struck Friendswood, and the "wet" side of Hurricane Harvey opened up full force for a second flood. Family members woke up before dawn to two inches of water in Chris and Marti's house. Immediately, the task of pushing water out began as the rain eased enough to stop the flooding.

The slate and wood floors were swept, cleaned with a Shop Vac, and towel dried. The wet carpet was pulled up. The family counted this another happy day because the head count was correct; all the people and pets were dry.

A quick follow-up note: Remember the policeman friend who spoke with Rob on the bridge? Two weeks after the storm, Rob saw the same policeman again as he was riding his spare motorized chair on the road. The policeman stopped him to ask, "Where you been? Last time I saw you, you were sitting on the side of a flooded bridge. Why didn't you check in with us?"

All the local policemen are Rob's friends. They watch over him as he rides his scooter next to major roads back and forth to work every day. It's always nice to have friends in high places whether they wear silver badges or gold halos!

XXII
A Word of Thanks
by Chris Barden
(as told to Patricia Vance)

Our family is eternally grateful for all the prayers and encouragement, plus the outpouring of labor-intensive help with the jobs of destruction/gutting to construction/rebuilding of four houses.

"Mucking out" the wet sheetrock to open up the walls was absolutely urgent to get these four houses dry and to prevent mold. Roving crews of workers with sledgehammers knocked on doors and offered to tear out the wet mess and haul out the trash. Friends (present, past and new) came to help from as far away as San Antonio and Atlanta.

So many volunteers -- non-flooded neighbors, churches, high school sports teams, family and complete strangers -- just came by, rolled up their sleeves and, out of the goodness of their hearts, did whatever needed to be done. Even money was given to provide much-needed assistance.

These heroes gave of themselves for months, with ever more work from pulling up the once beautiful, glued-down but now warped, hardwood floors to ripping out kitchen cabinets. You name it: They did it.

An unsung helper was Jan, a silver-haired grandma from our grandson's preK church school, who worked harder and stronger hauling logs than even an elephant would have. Amazing!

Their generosity abounded. It was simply breathtaking to see the Golden Rule and Love Thy Neighbor put into action by so many of God's angels. Support is so important after this kind of emergency, as it heals the broken heart of loss.

And food. There was so much food donated that Marti didn't have to cook supper for almost three months. To all the cooks: Thank you! That was a special blessing as there were so many mouths to feed. Marti must have felt like a red cardinal Momma Bird with so many chicks in the nest. (These beautiful birds adore her backyard).

To the big truck driver who picked up Ashley and her family from their flooded house… And to our son's backyard neighbors, Susan and Bill, who sheltered us until we could be pick up… We send out a big THANK YOU!

There's a special warm and loving thanks to Christopher's friend Johnny Franklin and the two men with a boat – who remain unknown to us -- for help in the bridge rescue. "Beyond grateful" is not adequate for their generosity.

On behalf of the Barden/Armstrong family, all that we can humbly say in our true hearts' appreciation is: Thank You - We Love You!

XXIII
The Storm
Author unknown

On the morning of August 27, 2017, an internal storm woke me up. Internal storms seemed to recur in my life. I was depressed and desperate for God to pull me once again out of a raging internal storm. Little did I know how my world was about to be turned upside down by an external storm called Harvey.

That morning, I sat down and began to write what I believe He had to say to me, and I remember feeling Him lift me out of that internal storm as He was writing to me. And I think now that it was so neat how He used Harvey as an analogy of what was going on inside of me.

(His message to me, which I call *The Storm,* is transcribed at the bottom of this story, just as I wrote it down.)

That morning as I sat at my desk, the weather forecast for our area in Houston was for some possibly heavy rain, beginning that night. We were on the "dirty" side of Hurricane Harvey. So people were stocking up on supplies in case we lost electricity.

At 10:00 pm that night, the rain began. It was not a heavy rain at first, but then it began coming down heavier and heavier. I remember going to bed around 11:00 pm and thinking, "Perhaps I will get back up in a little while to check on the storm."

My husband was already in bed but got back up soon after I came to bed. It was about midnight when I got up to check on why my husband hadn't yet come back to bed.

I will never forget the moment I opened our front door to see how much rain we were getting. The water was making its way onto our front porch and quickly coming to meet me at our front door. At that moment, my husband and I realized that we might have a serious problem very soon.

I went to my son's room and told him to come out and see what was happening. He was 12 years old and about to experience an event that he would never forget and that would change his life.

I began scurrying around the house, gathering blankets and putting them in the doorways. What a crazy idea that was. No blanket was going to prevent the water from inviting itself into our home.

At one point I went to the back door that led to our patio and, as I opened that door, I was met by dozens of spiders rushing towards me to get away from the water that was quickly rising behind them.

Now, you need to know that I am terrified of spiders. And these were some creepy-looking specimens, like wolf spiders.

I screamed and slammed the door. I ran to get our industrial bug spray because I knew that when that water came in, the spiders would be coming in with it. They were already starting to come under the door. I reopened that door and started spraying the heck out of those spiders. There was no way those spiders were coming into my home. Oh, how I still get an eerie feeling when I see the image in my mind of those spiders rushing towards me.

By 1:00 am, the water began coming into our home. We began to run around frantically gathering electronics and other valuables to put up high on our counters, tables and other surfaces.

At one point, the rain slowed down and the water began to

recede a little. We had some hope that perhaps that was the worst of it. It wasn't!

Soon, the rain began coming down again with a fierceness I had never experienced before and still hope never to experience again. The water came into the house more powerfully than before, and it kept rising. It was to be one of the longest nights of our lives.

We were fortunate to not lose our electricity as we walked around in over three feet of water. I don't know what we would have done if we had no light. My husband, who has one leg due to an accident many years ago, was only able to walk around on his crutches. His prosthetic had to be put up high to protect the electronic components in it.

There was nowhere to go and no way out of this situation. We had to wait, pray, and wait some more. We were forced to put our two cats and two dogs on the kitchen table because the water was too deep for them to walk.

As daylight began to make its way to us, the rain was still coming down relentlessly. A slight panic began to sink in as we realized that we had to do something to get out of this situation. We couldn't sit in this water any longer. We had neighbors across the street who had a two-story house, and I knew I was going to have to walk across and ask them if we could come over and bring our animals with us.

I walked out the front door and, as I got closer to the street, the water came up to my shoulders. It was difficult to walk with the current in the water and the rain continuing to add to it. I remember telling myself, "Don't think about what might be in this water. Just walk."

Once I got to the neighbors' house, they were very welcoming and said we could all come over, including our animals. Now I had to figure out how I was going to get everyone over here, especially my husband. It was going to be very dangerous for him to walk through that swirling water with one leg and crutches.

I walked back to our house and began looking for ways to get our animals and son across first. Thankfully, the Lord gave me the idea to use one of our swim floaties. So I put the two cats in a carrier and put them on the floaty. Then I added our two dogs in a plastic storage tub. I decided to take our son with me so he could hold onto the floaty as he walked with me and the animals.

We got them across and unloaded, and now it was time to see how I was going to get my husband across.

But God already had the plan for us. As I walked out to go back across the street, a young man in a kayak came floating up to us. He said he was taking people up to the entrance of our subdivision where there was no water. Praise the Lord!

He went over to our house and loaded my husband onto the kayak. You have no idea what a relief it was to both of us. We were getting out of there, thanks to one selfless man who didn't even live in our subdivision. He just came to rescue people.

By the time we all reunited and got to the front of the subdivision, we were cold and exhausted. We had to wait a little longer to get someone to give us a ride out of there, but we knew we were fortunate to have a place to go nearby. Our nephew and his wife had a large house just a few miles away which had not flooded.

The next month was an emotional whirlwind, but we experienced God's love and provision in ways we never had before. Although we lost a lot of our belongings, including two vehicles, God replaced everything and upgraded us to even better than what we had before. We felt and experienced the love of God through all the people He sent to help us. It was remarkable!

It was no coincidence that, on that morning, God had spoken to me regarding my internal storms and, that night, He sent the external storm that would come and change my life.

I would go on to share *The Storm* with almost everyone I knew and even with some I didn't know. One gentleman who read *The Storm* called me to tell me personally how the writing had spoken to him and how he had it sitting on his desk to see every day. What a blessing it was to hear that.

Now I can say, "Thank you, God, for the storms in my life." I pray that, if you aren't able to say that yet, one day you will be able to.

May the following message, *THE STORM,* bless you.

THE STORM

My Dear Child,

I am here to calm the raging storm inside of you. Remember, I live in you, and I know what is going on inside of you. It does not matter to Me if you or something beyond your control creates the storm you face, I love you! No matter how catastrophic it is and how big the damage it creates, I am here! I will not leave you nor forsake you!

I see beauty through your storm. I see the pearls that are floating in your raging sea that will be brought to the surface one day. There is beauty in the ugliness of your storm. The beauty that, at times, only I can see. You must trust that the beauty is there even though you feel that it sometimes goes away.

You are sitting in the middle of Harvey, and this external tropical storm is similar to the one on the inside of you right now. I know that you feel like your internal storm is so slow moving that it will never pass, just like Harvey is doing now. Harvey is stalling above your community, pouring its rain on your cities, and no one knows how long it will last. But I do! It will pass.

The storm that rages upon the city of your heart will not always be there. I have the power to calm the storm, to stop the storm and move it along. This internal storm has a purpose: It stirs up what is settled deep inside you and brings it to the surface. I want the sediment at the bottom of your heart washed away for good. You may have many storms, My Child, but you must trust Me to reveal what needs to be washed away.

Destruction is not always a bad thing in a storm. If not for destruction, things could not be rebuilt. They could not be made fresh and new. Destruction is a necessary element in this life. Right now, destruction of self-sufficiency is what I desire to be washed away. Destruction of your will must come crumbling down! How else can I do that but by a storm? Sometimes it takes a tropical storm, and sometimes it takes a category five hurricane to destroy self-sufficiency.

Trust that the storm is serving its purpose. I will use all the storms in your life to bring about good for you and for My purposes. When you sense a storm is coming on, when you have warning, check with Me. I am your radar. I will either help you prepare for the storm or stop the storm.

I love you so much! I care so deeply about all the constant storms going on inside of you. You don't have to live in this constant state of trying to keep the storm at bay and then having it come on top of you. I desire to help you sidetrack many of the storms by giving you My peace, My comfort, and My sustaining power.

I love you! I have just calmed the storm in you. Do you feel it? I know you do. Now, let it subside and have peace.

Love,
God

Psalm 107:29 (NIV) He stilled the storm to a whisper; the waves of the sea were hushed.

XXIV
Harvey Versus Dian
by Dian Stirn Groh

Advertised and touted for weeks by meteorologists, this battle of Mother Nature against Mankind set records around the world. This "Fight to the Finish" will long be remembered. Following is the play-by-play:

Introducing: In the West Corner, packing winds of 80 mph, the Big Brawler (i.e., the aggressive fighter who throws many punches on the inside) named Hurricane Harvey. While basically a scrawny storm, it is a plodder (i.e., a slow fighter who consistently pushes forward), which will drop 50 inches of rain over six days in one spot. And that spot is Dickinson, Texas.

Introducing: In the East Corner of that town, Dozing Dian, who lives on a retention pond that backs up to the Green River, which then feeds into Gum Bayou, Dickinson Bayou and Galveston Bay. Mind you, her house has never flooded before, and water has come up slowly during the first two days of rain in this instance. There is even a break in the pounding long enough for her to attend a surprise birthday party for a friend on Saturday, August 26th.

After the party, however, Harvey redoubles his efforts. The rains come down and text messages fly through the airwaves. Late Saturday, the notification goes out: Church service is canceled for Sunday. Dian thinks this is overcautious because the river has not even spilled out of its banks to join her pond yet. When the two had become one on several other occasions in the past, there had been no negative impact (i.e., no flooding), so she continues to feel safe.

Dian hears the wind and rain but remains calm and sleeps well.

However -- she is caught cold (i.e., like a boxer who gets hurt in the opening rounds because she is not mentally or physically prepared). Harvey is now a contender for "championship hurricane" and is relentless. He attacks with a vengeance all night long.

Upon waking at 7:30 am on Sunday, August 27, Dian is doubled over temporarily with a gut-wrenching jab to her house. Putting her feet on the floor results in "squish, squish, squish." During the night, Harvey's continuously pelting rain has seeped into her home to cover the baseboards and soak the carpet, walls and insulation.

In the front yard, water is flowing freely in the street and reaches almost to the top of her brick mailbox.

Dian Groh's front yard on August 27,2017 at 7:41 am
Photo courtesy of Dian Groh

In the back yard, the scene isn't much better. The water level has reached the top cross-rail of her four-foot wooden fence.

Dian Groh's backyard with the Green River overflowing its banks on August 27, 2017 at 9:20 am
Photo courtesy of Dian Groh

As Dian prepares to leave, her pit-bull pup Stormy baulks at walking in the water, so Dian avails herself of a metal rowboat a neighbor has left as he drove his family to safety in his work truck. Only a block away, the houses are high and dry, but the water is about three feet high in the street.

Although there is no bell to end this round of the fight, Harvey holds off his attack. Dian takes a break and stays with a neighbor overnight.

However, Harvey Hurricane isn't finished with her by any means. In Round Two, the rains resume with redoubled fury. Although her car in the garage has wet tires, it is still in good shape and starts easily when the water recedes somewhat.

The uppercut comes when Dian attempts to comply with the mandatory evacuation of her neighborhood and tries to reach her daughter in Pearland. Loading her pit bull, clothing thrown into several bags, and everything she could fit in a cooler into her car, she sets out. League City Parkway (FM 96) is the only passable road under I-45 and even that is chancy, with huge trucks zipping along and throwing up spray high enough to cover her windshield. She and Stormy are breathing heavily with concern, which makes the windows repeatedly steam up and impede her vision. Guided by directions from her daughter (with many impasses and false starts), she tries to dip and dodge the flooded roads, with water covering the curbs in most places.

To make matters worse, the car has no air conditioner. Even with the windows open only a crack, the rain is coming in sideways. So fresh air is not to be had.

Blindly, Dian slugs her way toward Maple Leaf Drive and to Friendswood Drive (FM 518), still edging north, but Harvey takes the upper hand by creating an impasse at Chigger Creek, so high that even jacked-up trucks turn around, unable to ford the river that is flowing across the road.

Is our weak contender done for?

With her daughter directing her via cell phone, Dian rallies. She digs deep and intensifies her efforts to reach Sunset Drive, the back entrance into her daughter's neighborhood. She is now so close that she can almost taste victory. And yet, Sunset is also blocked by rushing water.

Still receiving strategies and moves via cell, she is forced to turn around and seek other routes through unknown neighborhoods. Then, with only two miles to go, at the urging of people out in the rain, she proceeds to the intersection of Edinburgh and Essex in Friendswood.

There Harvey throws his last devastating below-the-belt punch and saturates the car to the top of the tires. With Dian holding her breath and keeping her foot on the gas, the car gasps and quits in the middle of the intersection.

For a while, sadly, it looks like Harvey wins. Is she defeated? Not Dian!

Miraculously, four teen-age boys from her neighborhood suddenly come out from nowhere and push the car up into an elevated driveway. One opens her door and says, "Come on, get out. You can stay with us."

The rescue boat traveling on Green Isle Avenue when the rain stopped. Taken on August 27, 2017 at 10:17 am
Photo courtesy of Dian Groh

Dian responds, "You'd better ask your parents about that."

He said, "My dad already said we could take someone in."

"But I have a big dog."

"That's okay, we have two big dogs."

Dian feels that she may win this bout after all. She stays with the generous Downs family overnight, provides a plank of salmon for dinner from her evacuated freezer, and licks her wounds.

Dian Groh's dog Stormy on the sofa not wanting to get her feet wet. Taken on August 27, 2017 at 8:00 am
Photo courtesy of Dian Groh

Though bruised, battered and worn out, Dian's rescue is the beginning of her bouncing back. When she returns home, strangers help to pack up her clothing, move flooded furniture to the street, muck out her house, and cut out the rotten drywall. Other new friends help move salvageable items to storage.

She has been shucking and jiving, bobbing and weaving, perhaps swinging wildly at times, but she will be triumphant in the long run. There may be mental scars, but she will survive the fight.

Harvey may have inflicted pain and agony but like "the Unsinkable Molly Brown" from the *Titanic*, Dian ain't down yet!

XXV
Losing My Beloved Sanctuary
By Pat Bradshaw

I have heard that a story should not begin with, "It was a dark and stormy night." But….

It was a dark and stormy night. The rain pummeled down, forcing thousands of gallons of water to pile up as the thunder rang out in the heavens. Filling the low areas, the water had no way to escape. As an uninvited guest, it intruded into the peaceful sanctuary of my home.

No, I did not expect this intruder to violate the perimeters of my dwelling place. Nor did I expect it to stay so very long. It was one thing for this water to intrude into my home uninvited, but it was the length of time it tarried that forced this disastrous ordeal upon me.

I specifically remember the day, not that this has anything to do with the hurricane other than the irony of it all. August's blistering heat was in full bloom. I had decided to take my stand against the heat, so I put on my bathing suit and joined my neighbors in our pool for an exercise class. This firmly imprinted the day in my memory, mostly because it was the first and last time that I sought out the pleasures of immersing myself in that swimming pool.

Surviving August's scalding heat is always a deep concern for me. At my age, breathing becomes a difficult chore in temperatures above 80 degrees. Now we were well into August, when the temperatures (hovering in the 90's) made me weary of being any place without air conditioning. Thus, my greatest fear throughout this ordeal was the loss of electricity.

However, God's blessing abounded, and my fear was unfounded. Walking through this entire trial, I never lost electricity. I feel very blessed because of that.

However, even as the storm began, I was no stranger to the unwelcome intrusion of water in my home. Water had complicated my move into a new apartment less than a year earlier, when the refrigerator sprang a leak the night before move-in day. When the movers arrived the next morning, they had nowhere to put my belongings that was not wet.

Complicating things further, maintenance men, carpet-replacing people, water-restoration people, office personnel, along with numerous of my family members and friends were crowding into my tiny apartment, each trying to resolve some part of my first flood.

Only a few short months later, without my knowledge, the water from the kitchen sink overflowed and filled parts of my apartment. Mopping and sopping up water was becoming a part of my life – a part I could gladly do without.

Thus, as midnight approached on that hot August day in 2017, I looked around my nice little home and noticed water creeping in under the doorway. Not wanting to get upset (as you can understand I'm quite used to water in my home), I called the apartment office.

Shortly after my call, three guys poked their heads through the door. All I remember is the big guy saying "Mrs. Bradshaw, you have got to sit down." Since I happen to be an elderly lady and have a fear of falling, I did as he suggested…for a while.

However, several days went by before I saw him again. I wondered how many days I was supposed to just sit there in all that water. If I had done as he said and sat there doing nothing... well you can imagine, things could have been worse.

So Harvey brought me my third flood in less than one year. (I was becoming familiar with the process.) But this time, trying to sweep the water out the door was not working because that was where this intruder was coming from.

My second option...I began sopping up water with towels. At my age, wringing them out was not possible. So I took a little journey down the hall where I enlisted the help of the washing machines to wring them out.

But I realized that this water was not like the water of my two previous floods. They were both clean water that was drinkable before being on the floor. This water was from who-knows-where and contaminated with who-knows-what.

The office called a water extraction company and was surprised to find out there would be at least a three-day delay in getting to us. Not because of the magnitude of jobs but because the roads were impassable: There was high water everywhere.

Things probably would have been okay if someone could have gotten the water removed that night or the next day. But as it turned out, I sat there for a week, sloshing around in the contaminated water as it soaked into the walls and floor.

Finally, I was required to vacate my home in order to have it repaired. The office people did their best and located a hotel room nearby. However, the first room was without handicap facilities, which I required. Showering was impossible and navigating through the room was not easy.

Everyone who was flooded was looking for a place to stay. It took some doing, but the office located another room which had the necessary facilities for me to get through a day. This hotel made dealing with the ordeal bearable, and I was grateful.

I also found great comfort in my Facebook friends throughout this time. Some of them were dealing with circumstances far worse, yet they were posting words of encouragement to all who were struggling.

My friend Pastor John, whose house was completely under water, had many encouraging things to say. How could I be discouraged? What I was dealing with, although traumatic to myself, was only a fraction of his story.

Another friend, Doug the evangelist, whom I have not seen in years, shared inspiring and encouraging words that really helped me through this difficult time.

Pat Bradshaw sitting on her hotel bed after Hurricane Harvey
Photo courtesy of C. Chapman

In the meantime, my dear friend Cathy, along with my children and grandchildren wanted to help me. Poor old Granny. Unfortunately, their efforts were in vain since they all lived on the other side of Clear Creek. I imagine that my children were worrying about me more than I. I thought it was all pretty interesting.

When I was living in the hotel after Hurricane Harvey, I heard many heart-wrenching stories from others staying there. Some had to be evacuated by boat from their homes. Others were displaced quite a distance from family and friends.

My blessing abounds in not being able to include such trials here. Their stories would probably be more shocking than mine. However, this was enough for this lady to endure.

XXVI
Hurricane Season is Here: Be Prepared
by **Rev. Kathy Sebring**

A few days before Hurricane Harvey, I received a phone call from a member of my congregation. "How are you getting to church on Sunday?"

Thinking this was a strange question, I replied, "Same way I do every week, I'll take I-45."

Her reply was quick. "Have you looked at the weather report?" Obviously, I hadn't.

My first anniversary as the pastor of First Presbyterian Church in Dickinson was that coming Sunday. In addition, I was also a novice when it came to hurricane preparedness, moving from California to Houston after Hurricane Ike. Earthquakes, I knew: Hurricanes, zilch.

Disbelief overwhelmed me as I watched Channel 13 to see boats motoring between the church's front sign and its stained-glass window. (The bottom of the window is approximately six feet from the ground.) Would there be anything left of the church?

Looking back, there was no way to really prepare for Harvey. Sure, do the normal -- get gas, food, medicines, prepare to evacuate. These preparations helped -- some.

I remember calling two organizations that First Presbyterian Church of Dickinson regularly helped with diapers and baby wipes. "Come get your supplies, they are in our narthex and might get wet…. You might need them before we can get them to you."

Boy was that an understatement! One of our affiliates, UTMB-

Kid Launch, opened their doors and were greeted with sodden diapers as big as beach balls floating everywhere. For us, a pair of brass candlesticks, our big Bible, a communion table, and diapers (stored in the balcony) were the only things to survive Hurricane Harvey.

The interior of First Presbyterian Church of Dickinson,
with the sun shining through the stained-glass window
in the aftermath of Hurricane Harvey
Photo courtesy of Rev. Kathy Sebring

Devastation caused by over four feet of water in our lovely church was heartbreaking. A struggling church to begin with, Harvey could have been the death knell for First Presbyterian Church of Dickinson.

But that was not to be the case. In fact, the outpouring of help, inspired by the Holy Spirit, has given new life and purpose to our church.

An ice machine and debris in the yard of First Presbyterian Church of Dickinson in the aftermath of Hurricane Harvey
Photo courtesy of Rev. Kathy Sebring

When we were finally able to get to the church, we found our front door blocked by a fishing boat, a picnic table, and an industrial ice freezer (belonging to the gas station on the other side of the freeway).

We pried open the doors and were met with snakes and fish swimming out the front door -- along with my theology books. This was when even the strongest of heart might have cried "Uncle." But God had a plan for us.

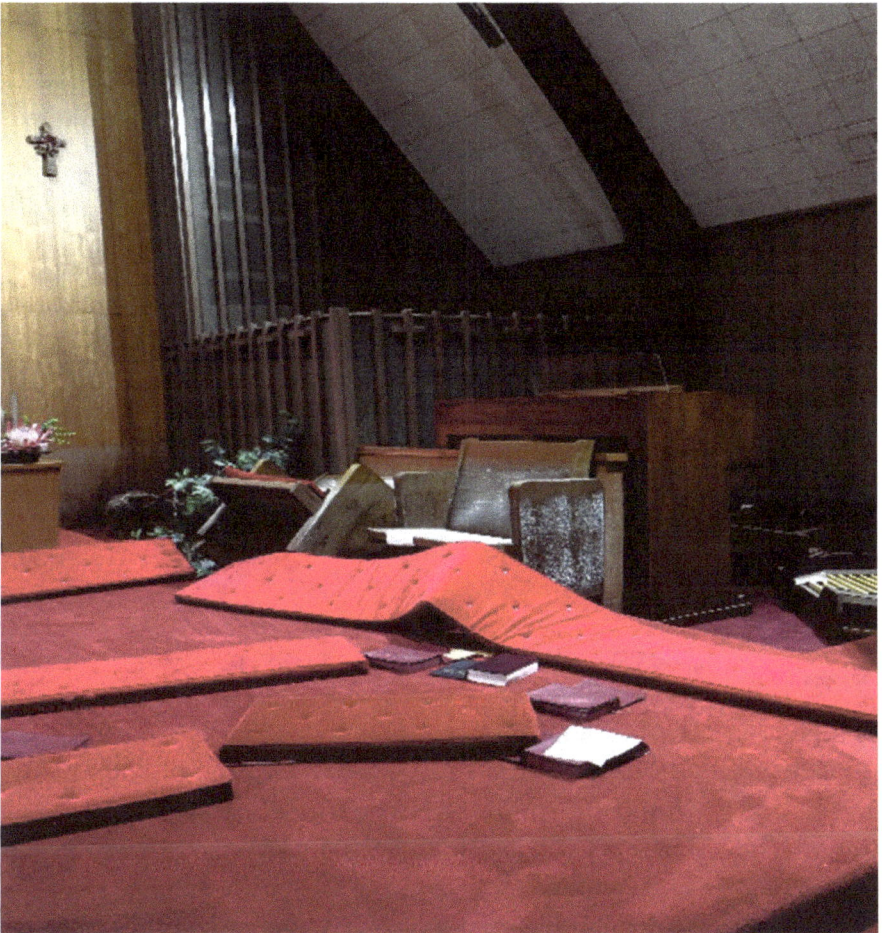

The debris-filled interior of First Presbyterian Church of Dickinson in the aftermath of Hurricane Harvey
Photo courtesy of Rev. Kathy Sebring

On the second day, people began to arrive. Over 60 "good souls" came to muck out and clean up. People from Clear Lake, Texas City, Webster and around the country came to help. Fuller Center for Disaster Rebuilders repaired the heating and air-conditioning, gutted and put back the bathrooms, and de-molded the ceiling.

In three days, the sanctuary was gutted with all debris removed.

A debris-filled office at First Presbyterian Church of Dickinson
in the aftermath of Hurricane Harvey
Photo courtesy of Rev. Kathy Sebring

Barely had the debris been removed, when an 18-wheeler from Louisiana full of survival supplies pulled into our parking lot. On borrowed shelves, pallets and tables, the supplies were stacked and ready for distribution. When we were done, over 640 people had received food, clothing, diapers, cleaning supplies, etc.

On the heels of this relief effort came a call from SAS/San Antonio Shoes, "We want to give people shoes. Can you help?" Once again, we opened our gutted sanctuary and hosted the biggest shoe giveaway SAS had ever done in one day. Over 1800 people received 2000 pairs of shoes, T- shirts and socks. The constant stream of people lining up for supplies and shoes over the weeks reinforced our belief that we were alive and in the business of being Christ's hands and feet to our community.

Every church on FM 517 had sustained damage, and all of them found other places to worship. We stayed -- on the lawn -- visible to all who drove by.

The first Sunday after Harvey was Communion. With borrowed Communion cups, plates, chairs and visiting college students providing music, we held worship. The Lord's Supper, prayer and hope were given to all who stopped by.

The media even came: *The Houston Chronicle* published an article, *The New York Times* photographed our service, and the pictures were relayed to other papers across the country. Our service streamed on Facebook.

On the first-year anniversary of Harvey, the *Chronicle* did a follow up story. Individuals, churches, and other organizations have continued to help our various ministries: the Christmas Closet, "Cheery Cheeks" (diaper ministry that helps 85 families and over 200 infants), gift cards for sundries and building supplies, and the quilt ministry.

Church groups traveled to Dickinson to help with projects. One group of young people came from First Presbyterian Church in Mesquite, Texas. The L.I.F.E (Living in Faith Everyday) bell and youth choirs led worship with beautiful music. They also redesigned and planted the Memorial Garden, and did other heavy work that was beyond our capabilities.

Harvey brought devastation and grief, but when I marvel at the wonders and miracles God has given us (and to others through us) because of the storm, I am humbled.

I am reminded of John 15, about the vine and the branches. Through Harvey, God cut off a lot of dead branches. No doubt, He pruned us. Clutter was swept away, sacred cows were discarded, the deadly "We've always done it that way" attitude is completely gone. Hope is strong, recognition of God's hand in our recovery is on everyone's lips. (We were told our A/C might last a few months because of the damage. Five years later it is still working!)

We are alive and well, under construction, challenged but not daunted. Lacking FEMA aid, recovery has been slow (construction on the bathrooms and a new entry will begin in the summer of '22.)

First Presbyterian Church of Dickinson is alive and moving forward. The lights are on. Our stained-glass windows can be seen clearly in the night. It is obvious that God's people are at home.

We are open and welcoming to all.

By Rev. Kathy Sebring, Pastor of First Presbyterian Church Dickinson, TX.

www.1stPresbyterianDickinsonTX.org

XXVII
Harvey Guilt
By Maureen Cullen

I remember the time of Harvey well. Not because of any damage or discomfort I suffered, but because it coincided with my much-anticipated vacation to Ireland. Wanting to shorten the flight to Europe, my friend Karen and I flew to Boston on August 24th to meet my other two friends from Maine. Had we not done that, I would never have been able to leave. We left for Boston on Thursday and everything with Harvey started on Friday. We were very fortunate to miss Hurricane Harvey.

My husband and daughter who stayed here in Seabrook, however, experienced the storm first-hand

My daughter is a teacher in HISD and, although she has an apartment across town, she stayed at our house during this whole episode. My husband is an engineer for Dow in Deer Park and was not able to go to work for two weeks.

They did not expect anything much to happen with the storm because no one had told them to evacuate. It wasn't "Here is this big Hurricane Ike, you need to get out." It was different.

My husband and daughter kept in contact with me and let me know what was going on with the storm.

Harvey even made the news in Ireland: It was reported that there was bad flooding in Houston. Being so far away and in the middle of a wonderful vacation, it was difficult for me to grasp what the people at home were dealing with.

My friend who was with me in Ireland had boarded her dog in League City. As we heard about the flooding and worried that her dog might drown, she wanted to get in touch with the kennel. She spent at least two agonizing days trying to get through to them. When she did get in touch, she found out everything was okay.

Her son works for the City of League City, and she was able to get in touch with hm. So she knew some of what was happening. Her son drove one of the trucks back and forth to rescue people stranded on a League City bridge.

This was a very clear example that, when there is an awful event (even if you are not directly in the middle of it), not being able to get in touch with those you care about is part of the trauma.

Even though I kept in touch with my family, I had no idea what had really happened. Because I was not personally involved, I didn't really have a grasp on how bad it was.

I came home 12 days after Harvey hit. Nothing was destroyed or flooded in my house, but we kept seeing news stories of all the people who were having to muck out their houses.

I am very proud of my husband because one of the things he did while he couldn't work was to help other people muck out their houses. I also remember how proud I was that he contributed to the J.J Watt Fund to help people devastated by the storm. J.J. Watt raised $37,000,000 in about three days. I hope this will be a learning experience for people that we need to search for opportunities to be good and do good all the time, not just when bad things happen.

Ever since my daughter started teaching school, we take a picture of her first day of the school year in order to commemorate her teaching years. These pictures are usually taken on August 24th or August 25th. When I went to frame her third-year picture, I couldn't find it, until I realized her school didn't start until September 12th that year due to the storm.

Because I was on vacation and my house suffered no damage, I have what I call "Harvey Guilt." I couldn't do anything at the time because I was gone: I wasn't there. And, in any case, I don't have the physical body to be able to help with the hard labor like mucking out a house.

But I needed to relieve this sense of "Harvey Guilt" when I returned, so I searched for ideas of how I could help.

Flood waters remained days after Hurricane Harvey left the area. This photo is the Palais Royal parking lot at I-45 and FM 517 in Dickinson. Remaining high water can be seen in the background, preventing people from getting around.
Photo courtesy of C. Chapman

I saw that many of my Facebook friends had lost everything. One of my daughter's co-teachers had lost her house. My friend, who is a principal in Baytown, had her house flooded in Dickinson. Another assistant principal I know in Houston lost her entire house.

So – no -- the flooding didn't affect me directly, but it affected people I care about. So I came up with my plan.

I cooked complete dinners for them. I fixed them care packages with things I knew they would need. I put a teddy bear in each package because in times like these you never know when someone just needs a hug or needs something to hang onto. I told them I was coming to see them and bring them a goody bag.

Often, I had to deliver it to them at work because they didn't have a home anymore. One friend was living in an RV in her driveway.

Another friend had to move her family into a 500-square-foot apartment several blocks from her home. They were a family of three staying in a second-floor apartment. They had no place to put things; even the microwave was on the floor. If they wanted to use it, they had to move things around and get it plugged in. I took them dinners from Valentine's Day until May 2018.

It took another friend a year after the flood just to get the permits to start rebuilding. It had taken two professional adults a year of haggling with the insurance company in order to even start to rebuild. Their problem occurred because the property value exceeded the house value. So even with flood insurance, things can be very difficult.

I readily admit I have more than enough PTSD over this. My husband has more than enough PTSD. We have lived in this area for 30 years, but now wonder if we can continue to live here.

We went thought Ike and Katrina. I remember Gilbert in 1988, when we were warned to evacuate and nothing happened. We are getting up there in age, close to retiring. Soon we will be in our 60's, 70's and 80's. I don't think we could go through something like Harvey at those ages.

A couple of things that I hope future generations can learn from this experience:

- Appreciate the good times when you have them.
- Be wise in looking for a home.
- Know where the flood plains are near you.

And be involved in your community so you know when they change the flood bonds. New construction can change the flow of drainage and cause areas that once stayed dry to flood.

So in closing I would like to leave you with two thoughts:

- Try to be kind to people more often. Just because. Don't wait for something bad to happen.
- And be real smart about living in a flood plain.

XXVIII
Don't Just Tell Me - Show Me
By Patricia Vance

A Letter to the Sweet Barden Family:

I think your extended family had some of the most interesting encounters I have heard about Hurricane Harvey. Remember when that's all everyone talked about? As the years go by, there will be fewer of these conversations. And before you know it, many of the details will be misplaced or rearranged or forgotten. Future generations should know - should want to know - what happened to their ancestors (by the way, that's us) during the storm. Maybe it's why ancestors.com is so popular.

How you felt during and after this event is so important. Your actions and their implied emotions make the story come alive and connect you to the reader's imagination. This moves the story beyond being just another documentary.

Your family shared in a heroic rescue effort. Your story will be part of the many flood stories of Hurricane Harvey which will now be preserved in a book, kind of like a diary that reads like a novel. You are all members of 2017's historic experience of "too much rain, in too little time, in too small a space."

I think your collective story of courage is huge and remarkable -- the right stuff that heroes are made of. I'm still amazed. And I'm glad that it will be told to people outside the Houston metro area who are interested in the power of such a large and destructive storm.

Most of all, I want to thank you for taking me into your home and letting me experience your assembled responses to all that

Harvey threw at you. It is something I will never forget. I saw supportive love in action between people who are related by blood or marriage. I saw how you act when faced with a major upheaval in your lives. You were all so brave, and you pulled together as one solid unit with each individual performing the necessary task at hand.

Of course, there were tears shed for serious losses initially, but your eyes were soon dried. Y'all moved forward one day at a time with one foot at a time. There were very few complaints: Everyone knew that accomplished nothing and drained much-needed energy.

Soon, there was a positive attitude in the air. Laughter was found in full supply and evenings were always a party. In the early morning, before time to go out and face another day of hard labor, breakfast was served. On the menu was delicious gourmet coffee with hot fluffy biscuits spread with real butter and dripping with honey. There was also Marti's homemade fig jam, made from the fig bush in her backyard. All was so yummy! The camaraderie nearly made cleaning up the messes in the family's three other flooded houses seem not so difficult after all. Well … almost!

When tested, your faith and actions rose to the occasion without a destructive, depressing "poor me". Instead, you all relied on the strength of Christ. A lifetime of loving and serving God really showed, and He generously replied. Selfless giving ruled, and it was a beautiful thing to watch.

The world desperately needs to hear good news that comes of a bad situation – like a silver lining inside a dark rain cloud. We have so few examples of people being members of a good and truly devoted family. Too many people have not had this experience.

Fear is behind the world's "bottom-line" question: "If this happened in my life, would I survive?" And "How did you do it?" They want to know how you felt when, out of left field, a big bad bully hit you in the gut with a mighty force. "How did you get back up to fight another round or go on another day?" Part of the answer seems to be an unspoken but shared battle cry of "Onward and Upward."

Are y'all perfect? No, of course not. No one is except the Lord. But you trust God and lean, not on your own understanding, but on Him. He's the center of your family life: Jesus is the answer that works!

To sum: All the most interesting stories follow the adage "Don't just tell me -- show me." Your story – and your family -- do just that!

P.S.

Marti and Chris Barden took me into their beautiful home and sheltered me there for three months. Their love is given to others through what we call "Southern hospitality" or the Lord's Gift of hospitality. Even though I was already a member of the family through marriage via my daughter Suzie, they made me feel like I was really a part of their family. Their acts of kindness and generosity helped me recover from the flood's trauma and extreme inconvenience. Both Marti and Chris refused any compensation.

Chris even drove me across Houston to look at a potential replacement for my brand new car that had drowned in three feet of water. He drove me when he was very tired after a long hard day of work repairing houses. He wouldn't take "we can do this later" for an answer, saying that the car I wanted might be snatched up, thus time was of the essence.

The best part of camping out at their "central headquarters" was getting to lovingly bond with Ashley's two children. Leah was so gracious in sharing her extra comfortable space. To this day, the kids give me a big hello and hug when we meet. I even learned to like living with five big dogs -- plus one little dog. They made great roommates!

Living under Chris and Marti's roof was a wonderful experience… one I will always cherish. It was lots of fun despite all the storm-caused hardships. I guess this can be called my "silver lining" to a huge out-of-control rain cloud labeled Hurricane Harvey.

The memories "flood" back to me at odd moments now. My daughter Suzie's husband (Christopher), rescued my Christian art paintings from destruction. He had the children run the many art canvases upstairs just minutes before the icky, brownish water busted its way inside the house.

When we evacuated from my house, Suzie held my arm as we waded through nearly two feet of high water in the back yard. We had to crawl through a pried-off open board in the fence to reach the neighbors' dry yard. Their house was at the front of the neighborhood and the flooded house was in the back cul-de-sac.

Throughout this storm-induced ordeal, Christopher and Suzie made sure I was cared for and landed on my feet, like a cat does when it jumps into the unknown.

They did the same by inviting me to live in their home when my husband, Patrick, her dad, had a major stroke in 2014. He lived in a nursing home for eight years. All three of my children (Travis, Sherry & Suzie) did not want me to live alone. Each did their part.

My son Travis also invited me to stay with him, but I was already well cared for. However, when time came to move into an apartment, he rented a truck and moved the metal shelves and wooden tables, etc. that had survived. He also picked up a donated dresser to fill in the gap. And he hauled my "million" art books that had made it safely through the storm on upper shelves. The books in plastic bins on the floor did not survive, as the swift-flowing water pushed these heavy boxes over. I was surprised by the excessive power of the water, even indoors.

A flooded neighborhood cul de sac.
Harvey did not recognize property boundaries.
Photo courtesy of Patricia Vance

Leah, Amy, Molly and their friends hauled all my drenched things to the massive, tall trash pile that covered the whole front yard. Whatever was still dry was added to a new stack on top of a table or in the driveway.

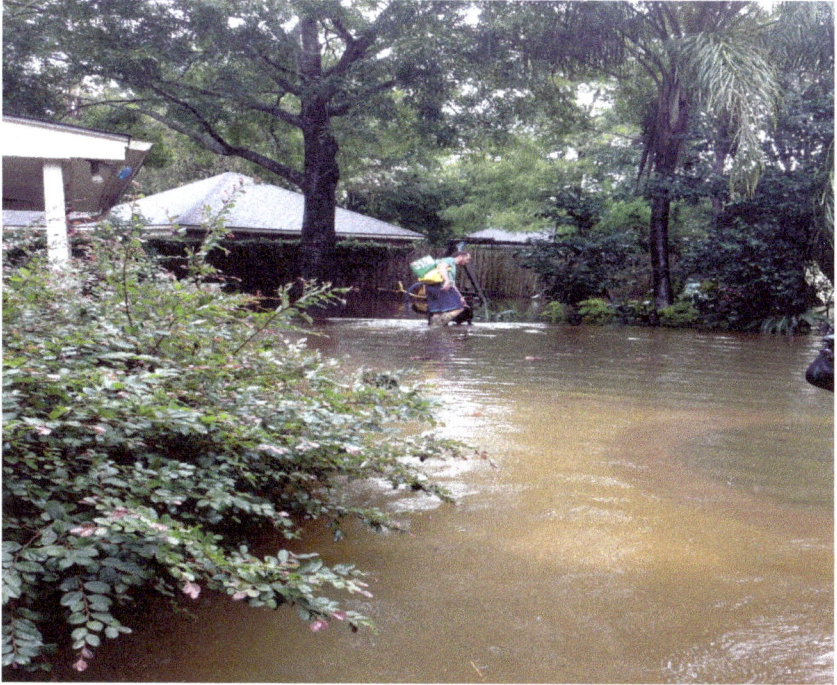

Chris Barden walking through his flooded backyard
to the neighbors' fence line with his two dogs
(the smaller one in his backpack)
Photo courtesy of Patricia Vance

My "French Cottage," as I called the living space in the flooded house, was about 85% lost. When I couldn't be there to mop up, Leah and Amy took care of my "stuff."

I have lovely family and friends who helped me clean up, box up, move up, move out, haul away, throw away, give away and whatever else I had to do to reorganize my remaining things to begin afresh. To name a few of them:

- My son, Travis
- My grandchildren: Jonathan, Cooper, and Kaley
- Friends: Panna, Raj, Lori, Vicky and Lorig, Anna's Ministry and others (even while most people were busy cleaning up their own disasters)

- My daughters: Suzie (who is local) and Sherry (who is a thousand miles away) who gave moral support and encouragement
- My friend Cathy, who gave me a brand-new mattress (which Suzie then picked up)
- And monetary donations from friends, family and even strangers

There was a group effort to overcome, survive and eventually prosper as before. That most unique storm called Hurricane Harvey was the catalyst. All who were available pitched in, doing whatever they could to make life better for the less fortunate. That's the way it is supposed to work. This weather tragedy revealed the "Love thy neighbor" in the heart of the city where lived one family in particular.

To whom do I owe the most gratitude? "And the winner is?... Envelope, please...."

Most of all, I am grateful to the Lord Jesus, Himself. He gave His strength and ability to press on and endure. He provided for my needs like He said He would in the Bible. Moving back in to my house was not an option as my French Cottage had to be gutted along with the rest of the downstairs. So He twisted Uncle Sam's arm to make sure I had another nice place to live – and even provided a country view of trees, deer and bayou right in the middle of the city. Thank you, my Lord!!!

Jesus spoke to the storm on the Sea of Galilee saying, "Peace. Be still." The winds and waves ceased. Thus, calm was made real.

> Harvey was a dirty dancer.
> But God knew how to waltz!
> Harvey made ugly 'out of tune,'
> Loud, ear-splitting noise.

But God made beautiful 'in tune,'
Quiet, ear-pleasing melodies.
Harvey left destruction in his wake.
But God left restoration in His Way.

Thank you to everyone with bunches of hugs and flower bouquets. I raise my crystal goblet to toast each one with my deeply felt love and appreciation!

Jesus loves you!!!

Love to all,
Patricia Vance

XXIX
A Surprise Came Knocking at the Door!
By Marti Barden
(as told to Patricia Vance)

It was 9:30 am on a lovely morning -- no rain -- hurray! The calendar said Wednesday, August 30th, the day after Harvey had "left the building."

Only Marti Barden and daughter Amy were at the family's central headquarters, Marti and her husband Chris' home. Everyone else had gone to survey their own post-storm dwelling, to check out other area storm damage or help with demolition of son Christopher's walls. All the children had also tagged along because they wanted to see what had happened to their houses and rooms and toys.

A knock on the front door and Marti peaked out to see who it was. A soldier, in full military combat uniform with all its mighty impressive gear. Behind him she could see three large tanks -- adorned with more soldiers -- parked at the end of the circular driveway that ran just beyond the front porch.

The soldier politely said, "Ma'am, we've come to rescue you. We understand there are nine adults and six children here at this house."

Marti's quick wit replied, "you've forgotten five dogs of which four are Labs."

Not missing a step, he said, "We've been told that you need to be rescued."

Marti's turn: "I can't imagine who called. We've never lost electricity and we've got plenty of food. Five of the adults staying here are off 'mucking out' a house. The roads are clear enough to get to the grocery store. I really appreciate it, but we don't need to be rescued."

The soldier replied, "Ma'am, if the storm comes back here and you flood again, we cannot come back to get you. This is a one-time deal."

To which she said, in thanking him again, "I understand, but there are a lot of others in need of rescuing. I heard airboats going down our street when it first flooded."

With Southern hospitality, Marti asked if the soldiers needed water or if they would like some cookies.

"No, we are ok," replied his nice voice.

And with a smile, she told him, "Well, thank you again for coming by. We are ok, too."

With that, he bid Marti goodbye and walked back to the tanks.

Since the tanks could not back up and go down the driveway to the street, they had to proceed forward on the semi-circular ribbon of concrete that lay between the house and a lovely flower bed.

Tanks are wider than cars -- kind of like comparing a German Shepherd K-9 dog and a 20-lb Terrier dog (which is the weight limit for most apartments). In both cases, size wins every time.

The waterlogged grass and mud along the curves of the driveway didn't stand a chance. The huge weight of the tanks dug in as they passed by the house. There was no other way out to the street.

The "Cajun Navy's" three Army tanks parked on this circular drive by the front door of Chris Barden's house.
Photo courtesy of Patricia Vance

While the bushes in the flower bed had a better survival rate, it had still been a hard couple of days for them. It's a wonder the greenery survived at all with the constant pounding. But a tree in the front yard was not so lucky.

All five dogs were in "hog heaven" and kept sounding the alarm as if announcing the parade of an invading army. This was the most fun they had ever had!

It's too bad the children weren't at the house to see the tanks and soldiers. They would have enjoyed seeing real tanks up close. Especially five-year-old grandson Vance Barden, as he loves huge metal moving machines.

Who knows, maybe the kids could have even been lifted by the soldiers to peer inside the tanks. Wow! It would have been exciting to say the least. Imagine -- the U.S. Army was here in the front yard of the house. This would be another storm story to tell that the children would never forget.

But now there was a mystery to solve. After much wondering and thinking over the last several days about who might have placed the call to the Cajun Navy for the rescue, the only clue came from daughter Leah. She had gotten a text message of concern from some distant friend who may have contacted the Cajun Navy from Louisiana. Then, the Cajun Navy may have contacted the Army to send the tanks because they couldn't get to the house. That's the only link anyone could think of. In either case, it was nice to know someone cared enough to arrange a rescue.

The soldiers had been stationed close by at a makeshift base in the parking lot of a fitness gym on FM 528, the major east/west road in Friendswood, which was flooded at the time. Only a tank was big enough -- and bad enough -- to sail through flooded streets and parking lots and circular driveways. Kind of like a 500-pound gorilla that goes wherever he pleases, especially when he has a backup plan that includes two more big gorilla buddies alongside.

Yet, through it all, Marti kept her cool. Growing up as the only daughter of a military officer, she knew just how to talk to a man in uniform.

XXX
The Amazing Spirit of Service after Hurricane Harvey
by Rev. Kyra Baehr

Who can imagine the devastation caused by 52 inches of rain within 36 short hours? Facts (supposedly true) that were shared through various media included comparisons such as "the volume of water was so heavy that the Houston metropolitan area sank slightly" and "the volume of water, if spread out, would be equal to two inches of water across all fifty states."

Whew. Those were just a couple of the remarkable statistics bandied about after Hurricane Harvey.

Hurricanes are well known considerations for those of us who live in the Gulf Coast region. When I moved here, I remember everyone saying I'd better prepare a "hurricane" kit or tub with potentially needed supplies, gathered and on-the-ready. The reactions to a hurricane warning range from the nonchalant to the pre-hurricane panic to *"hurry out of town"* and to the more stalwart *"I've weathered hurricanes in my home before, and I will weather this one from my home, too."*

There have been many times when an urgent hurricane warning of epic proportion ultimately fizzled into a small downpour or a few winds with no real significant storm effects other than a lot of media hoopla, a frenzy of filled sandbags, boarded-up windows, and a rush for water bottles at the grocery store.

Not so with Hurricane Harvey.

The unprecedented downpour of water inundated areas that

had never previously been flooded. The hurricane winds did not help, but the flooding around the hurricane zone, as it continued to pummel our community, was beyond my wildest imagination.

Unity Bay Area Houston is a small church community, ranging from 80 to 110 participants on most Sundays. We are just the right size for a very special religious experience as family. And did we ever experience that in the midst of Hurricane Harvey!

Unity Bay Area Houston serves parishioners in League City, along with many people from Webster, Dickinson, Alvin, Galveston, Clear Lake, Friendswood, Pearland, Kemah, Texas City, Santa Fe, San Leon and South Houston.

Around 35% to 45% of our regularly attending congregants lost homes and cars in the storm. Others lost financial means as jobs disappeared, or clients discontinued services. We worked to find temporary housing and to support many of them through these losses.

Emotional episodes of PTSD as well as overwhelming feelings of helplessness were triggered in some who had experienced past hurricanes and floods. After the first wave of panic passed, these emotional responses began and continued in waves. This was true not only of those who had been flooded and lost their family heirlooms and lifetime treasures, but also all those who served them. These support people experienced empathy, guilt (because they were safe and not personally impacted) and much more.

Our church became a center for connecting resources, providing cleaning supplies, and organizing volunteer teams for cleanup. We were also able to offer counseling services and on-grounds support for FEMA applications.

This debris pile, while not a recommended play place, served as the setting for a young Ninja's (Kaley Barden) imagination.
Photo courtesy of Patricia Vance

We have mostly a mid-life to older congregation, and they were quite amazing to behold. First-phase support involved hauling out flooded furniture and belongings, removing carpet and drywall, and help in sorting through what remained. Our 80-

and 90-year-olds were out daily hauling, cleaning, laundering, feeding, transporting, and supporting families whose homes had received between three inches and eight feet of water, as well as serving our local shelters and housing the evacuees. These were remarkable stories to share!

Many evacuees expressed fear of the unknown, as well as grief and shock at the devastation. Many have felt embarrassed, as their lives felt exposed and vulnerable when strangers (or even friends) dragged their belongings to the curb. Healing and rebuilding will feel like a long-drawn-out marathon even though the moment still feels like a full-on sprint. Adrenalin sometimes drove our volunteers until exhaustion set in. Then the need for self-care and balance for the long haul hit home.

There are many, many life-affirming stories of love and Divine order revealed in what some would call miracles. Christ Consciousness is embodied in every hand outstretched, every home opened with a heart of love, and every sandwich served. We are one family of humanity, and this was never more evident. The experience of oneness through shared prayers was undeniable. Many of our impacted church members received communications from long-ago school companions and workmates who reached out to check in, even though they had not spoken in 30 years.

Catholic Charities had people both inside our church and via a mobile unit to take FEMA applications and offer support and services.

Centers for Spiritual Living in Webster brought gift cards to share with families.

Lifeway International brought high school teens and parents to support our efforts, along with the coach and captains of the

Texas A&M Galveston Sailing Team & other sailing students.

Our congregants partnered with Clear Lake Regional Hospital on Tuesday to drive released patients through high waters to their homes so beds could be made available for others impacted by the storm. Some congregants drove doctors and nurses home after five days straight serving at the hospital. And some brought truckloads of cleaning materials and supplies from out of town the moment the roads were clear.

Our church, along with the Unitarian Universalist Church, Clear Lake Islamic Center in Webster, Interfaith Caring Ministries in League City and Interfaith Ministries of Greater Houston, all reached out in support of one another and the families we all serve.

The Crossing, a Pentecostal church community in Dickinson, used our facilities while recovering from their flood experience and determining where their community could move for further growth and fellowship.

Anita Kruse wrote a beautiful song titled "There Is More Love than Water in Houston" which was posted on YouTube. Her song, along with a video of first responders and rescue efforts, exemplifies the real experience here in our area. It is a message of hope, inspiration and heroic efforts. It is a message of #HoustonStrong!

Through it all, what we want to remember is how blessed and grateful we continue to feel for each person who we were able to hug again as we saw them safe and dry.

Divine messages are all around us, and our gratitude will continue to be shared as the more formal story of Hurricane Harvey is written.

XXXI
Caring for a Wounded Community
By Patricia Vance

The first morning after the heavy night rains that flooded so many homes, Calvary Chapel was still on dry ground. It became the drop-off point for rescue vehicles to unload their evacuated passengers. Unaware that they would need food for about 100 people on extremely short notice, the church did not have enough food on hand to feed a church mouse. But within a few days, it became the church with more than enough food. Calvary Chapel's parking lot hosted the Chefs of Hope Center in a manner similar to the "two fishes and a loaf of bread."

There were huge tents set up with lots of tables and chairs. Most important were the big containers with ovens and grills that could cook food right there on the spot. Food went to anyone and everyone who had no kitchen, to those who were helping to repair a kitchen, or to others who just needed a warm plate of food during or after a hard day's work.

While sitting at the table to eat, people would find that there was always someone else (usually a stranger) doing the same thing as them. They would mutually lend a comforting shoulder to cry on or an ear to listen. Without voicing it, they would feel a common bond and agree to say, "let's see the positive in this situation." And that usually led to a smile and maybe even a chuckle.

The fellowship of others in the same situation was warm and rich. Each person could truly say, "I feel your pain because I'm there, too." Understanding and compassion were freely given and received. Folks shared their new-found knowledge about how to survive a flood, how to repair a damaged house or what to do with a flooded car.

The Chefs of Hope travel near and far to set up after a disaster strikes. They do a remarkable job cooking (on site) large amounts of hot delicious, nurturing meals for those in distress. The church parking lot became the most popular new "restaurant" in town and their member volunteers worked tirelessly to make this project work smoothly. I believe that Chefs of Hope stayed in the area for about three months.

A big thank you from the hearts of all who were fed by Chefs of Hope and Calvary Chapel Church. Another big thank you to all the kind people who helped out where needed and wherever they could. Everyone worked together in harmony, as it should be.

This includes all the first responders and thousands of volunteers who helped those who were hurting. These are the very special people who care for their fellow man – those who they found beaten up by a terrible thief called "Harvey Storm." These unselfish folks became the Good Samaritans who treated and bound up the wounds of the innocent.

This is God's goodness: His measure of faith that we each receive that acts right toward and helpful to our fellow man's suffering.

Abraham Lincoln coined the phrase "the better angels of our nature" originally referring to the positive attributes of human character that he felt made the Union great. Now his famous words seem to mean the act of kindness – a gift from God.

XXXII
This Storm is not That Storm
by Kenyatha V. (K. Ellie Mae) Loftis

Her pacing is relentless, like the thundering of the storm outside. She's breathing heavily, first at the head of my bed, then at the foot—now back at the head. I can't ignore Nia any longer; I've tried really hard, perhaps to the point of neglect.

It's just a simple thunderstorm…. God forgive me for wanting a full night's rest.

"What do you want, Wookie? Are you hungry? Do you need to potty?"

She huffs and posts herself by my bedroom door. I can't see it in the dark, but I can hear the black tail swatting the air from left to right—now left again. If I don't make a move soon enough, she'll start scratching the door and wake my Mom. Now I huff, swinging my legs across the bed.

What good is a thunderstorm if you can't sleep through it?

I hear Nia reach her relief station, then drink loudly from one of her many water bowls. She stops at the other door, and I admonish her to "leave it!" and return to my room. She pauses and follows my lead. We lay down—me in my bed, she in hers—me hoping to take advantage of nature's sleep soundtrack. Just as I drift back to sleep, the pitter-patter on the roof becomes punctuated with … *panting.*

"Okay, fine," I exhale, climbing out of bed. I lift her with a quickness, trying not to lose too much of that sleep peace.

"Get in your spot."

She makes her way to the corner of the bed, and I am drifting back to sleep, until I hear the thud of her leap to the floor. Panting…. Then scratching on my door…. She wants out.

"No, Nia, let Ro-Ro sleep. She's very tired; she needs rest." But Nia is determined.

I open the door to my mother's room and lift Nia into the bed. She pauses to sniff at my mother's face and, satisfied that she is alive, heads to her spot. I return to my room, feeling a little guilty for punctuating Mom's rest with our intrusion, but more annoyed that Nia once again has foiled my plans for an uninterrupted night's rest.

Who doesn't want to sleep through a stormy night?

A bolt of lightning illuminates the familiar path between the rooms. I turn to close my door and there she is on my heels—panting again.

"What do you want, Nia?" I follow her back into my mother's room. I try to whisper so I don't wake my mother, "Everything's fine in here," as I lift her back into the bed.

I move toward my door and the panting follows.

"What's wrong, Wookie?" She tap dances back into the other room, where a lantern is now on.

"Sorry, Mom, Nia wants *something*." Content now that she has our attention, Nia marches us to the front of the house by lantern-light. She has food. She has water. Her relief station is now clean. We pause in the living room where all the furniture and things are still in disarray.

Then she marches us – again -- to my room. She leaps onto the futon and invites my mother to join her with her wagging tail. Mom sits, and Nia relaxes into her lap.

"You want me to sleep here, too, Nia?" Mom asks. Nia nuzzles in closer. "Okay, let me go get my blanket."

When Mom returns with her blankets and pillows, Nia disembarks the futon and burrows into her own bed. I look at the picture of us, a reprint of our "hunker-down" photo from six weeks ago. Mom was freshly post-operational and on medication that wasn't "too dangerous, but it *could* make her sleep too long," when Harvey arrived.

We had kept vigil on each other in this room, not knowing how or when the storm would leave us, sleeping through the turbulent nights and days—but not too long, and not too deeply.

This storm is not *that* storm. Yet, Nia seems convinced that *this* is how we weather a storm. She closes her eyes. Relieved.

XXXIII
Hurricane Harvey Saga
by Harold Raley

In late August of 2017 we spent several anxious days watching Hurricane Harvey dance along the Texas coast, hoping he would take his mischief elsewhere and let us get on with our normal affairs. But then, in just a matter of hours, Harvey ceased to be a red blotch on the television screen and came spinning his unwelcome way into Friendswood. Rains and wind started in our part of town in the late evening hours of Saturday, August 26, 2017, and continued throughout the night. By morning, after a mostly sleepless night for us, our garage was flooded and an hour or so later water was rising inside our home. The rain continued all day and by midafternoon on the 27th the water level had reached ten inches in the house and four feet or so in the street. We shut off the electricity, of course, though oddly enough, the electrical current stayed on throughout the storm in our part of town. The water maxed out an inch below our house plug-ins, sparing us the problem of wet electrical circuits during the cleanup.

At that point some good neighbors showed up in what appeared to be an odd gondola type of boat and offered to transport us to a neighbor's two-story house located across the street on higher ground than our residence. She generously offered shelter and refuge to us and another family in the flooded area. Her children were visiting relatives and she had plenty of beds and room. I believe someone snapped a picture or two of us doing our imitation Venice canal cruising.

By now the water had almost reached our neighbor's mailbox, four feet above the pavement. In the coming days it was the marker by which we monitored the water level, celebrating each dip and lamenting each rise.

Meanwhile, inside, dry and comfortable, we ate, talked of previous flood and storm experiences in Texas and elsewhere, and speculated on how long Harvey might prolong his stay and the damage he would do.

At one low point in the night with rain coming down in "Noachian" amounts, we discussed the possibility of leaving the comfortable house and trying to make our way across town to Friendswood High School, a designated shelter for flooded families. But after reminding ourselves how hazardous it would be to navigate—literally—our way in the dark and in rising, swirling water, we decided to stay put. A wise and welcome decision in my opinion.

If my memory is correct, the rains subsided for a time Sunday morning, and an hour later the mailbox marker showed a slight dip in the water level. Our spirits rose and we hoped that Harvey had done his darndest and was ready to move on.

I think, but am not certain of the sequence, that I waded across to our residence to assess the damage to our house. I was concerned of course about our two vehicles, one in the garage and the other in the driveway, and even more about the furniture, books, keepsakes, and papers in the house. In a word, everything.

I found what I expected: a soggy mess throughout the house and garage. And our swimming pool had become a polluted extension of Clear Creek.

As for the automobiles, the water was higher than I expected, and I was sure I was looking at two totaled cars. Actually, it turned out initially to be only one—my wife's vehicle—but about three or four months later my car also conked out with a bad transmission, damaged most likely by the water.

In any case, I waded back to our neighbor's house and reported the damage assessment to my wife and friends.

Then the rains commenced anew and continued hour after hour. We began to speculate again about leaving the house, for now the water was lapping only a few inches from the door. We were particularly concerned about the damage that would occur if the water came in, for our neighbor had just recently installed a new hardwood floor.

Eventually, about two inches of water did come in, just enough to do the dreaded damage to the beautiful hardwood. (Don't storms always aim for what we treasure most?) By that time our neighbor's children were due home, and my wife and I had moved into yet another neighborhood house around the block. I am not sure where the other couple went.

The second home was one we knew well and its occupants even better. They were old friends and made us feel as welcome and comfortable as did our first neighbor. We shall be forever grateful to both.

Somehow in the blur of events that followed, our daughter made her way down from Austin to help with the cleanup as soon as the storm cleared and we could get back in our house. She stayed with us at the second neighbors' house. She is a take-charge kind of woman with an expert eye for seeing the most effective way to solve problems.

A couple of days later, her brother—no less energetic than his sister—arrived from El Paso to spell her. Neither he nor his sister were bashful about putting their old Dad to work. And if the neighbors let me do very little, our offspring kept me busy throughout their stay.

My wife was occupied during the entire ordeal, for she had general oversight of the restoration, particularly the furniture, including some inherited classic sofas that had to be reupholstered, and conventional pieces that would have to be replaced.

The cleanup was epic, and I cannot begin to do justice to all the help we received from more generous neighbors and goodwilled folks than I can mention. Men, women and children pitched in and worked with an astonishingly high energy level. For example, I recall a stylish, refined lady mopping the floor after strong neighbors had removed the weighty, waterlogged carpet.

I meant to pitch in on several of these activities, but they would not even let me lift a box or man a mop. I was reduced mainly to watching and marveling at their generosity and intelligent plan of attack. If ever my faith in humanity wavered, it was restored with interest as I watched neighbors—and strangers—at work.

Meanwhile, Harvey carried his misery eastward, setting a record for rainfall over near Winnie, Texas, and leaving us with a mere 59 inches or so in Friendswood. I even had a twinge of disappointment when I heard the news. Couldn't the storm at least have set the record in Friendswood, thus giving us a topic of boastful conversation for years to come?

This neighborly campaign continued at the same pace for many days to come. People did laundry for us and placed furniture, clothing and other items in strategic order. I forgot to mention also that many folks brought their own tools, gloves, electric cables and connectors. When it was all over, we had enough donated batteries to last for years, with extra gloves, cables and tapes, some of which I was never able to identify and return to their owners.

As soon as I had time, I tackled the pool cleanup. It was full of unmentionable debris from Clear Creek. But I had an ace in the hole: my host neighbor who is a skilled engineer. With his guidance, and a daily regimen of draining and replacing the filthy water, we had the pool back to pristine purity a week later. Eventually, with the help of another great neighbor, I was able to replace the pool motors ruined by the water.

Neighbors - even strangers - helped us begin to rebuild
Photo courtesy of Harold Raley

Around that same time, we decided to move back home. Our neighbors protested that it was too soon, but we knew that they had gone out of their way to makes us welcome and comfortable.

We can never fully repay their kindness.

Piece by piece, everything fell nicely into place. We had an excellent FEMA inspector who responded in a timely way to our phone calls and questions—courtesies other flooded neighbors reported they had not always received. Not only was our inspector prompt, but also fair in his assessment of the loss. But all did not go smoothly. I shall sum up the aftermath of Harvey with the following experiences.

After the assessment was in and the financial amount due us was determined to our satisfaction, we had only to await delivery of the check. I tracked it by computer as it left Montana by plane, arrived in Colorado, then Kentucky, and finally in Houston by late afternoon. Then I followed it from League City as a FedEx truck distributed checks locally. Eventually the truck reached our neighborhood, made the rounds, and then, unbelievably, drove by without stopping at our house. By chance I knew the driver, and jumping in my still serviceable car, I caught up with his truck in South Pearland.

"No sir," he told me, "It's not in my truck. But I'll give you a private number you can call for information."

I called and was told—somewhat grudgingly it seemed to me—that several checks were mistakenly put on a truck going east out of League City. "But we'll deliver it later today," the person assured me. Later turned out to be around 9:30 pm when I saw a vehicle stop in front of our house, and a man came up the driveway with a flashlight and a package. He dropped the package and I quickly picked it up for him. It was the check, at last safely -- if tardily -- delivered.

Our good luck held in the following weeks as the final restorations were finished. I expected most of the money to go for basic repairs—sheetrock, doors, hardware, paint, carpet, etc., -- items in short supply in the area because of Harvey. But our contractor had expert ways of getting needed supplies. As a result, our house was finished well ahead of many others.

That meant we must now shell out a major amount—and maybe then some—for all the work. We were pleasantly surprised—you could say agreeably shocked—when the bill turned out to be a little over half of what we were expecting. So what happened?

The crew that did the work did not normally do restorations, but the owner told us that he had agreed to do four houses and that ours would be first on his short list. Many years earlier we had known him in his childhood and his parents as colleagues back in Oklahoma. We can only speculate, but never knew for sure, that he discounted the repair costs out of friendship. It was—so we believe—another noble act of generosity and good will that we experienced during and after the hurricane. In any case, it left us some money for a few other amenities and mitigated the financial hit that nasty Harvey had delivered.

Looking back, I must repeat all the accolades I said about our wonderful neighbors. For I am convinced that we live in one of the best neighborhoods and finest cities in this nation. At its worst, Nature can do dreadful things, but at its best, the human spirit can top them.

XXXIV
I'm Going to Stay
by Joanne Turner

September 29, 2018

My name is Joanne Turner. I was 63 at the time of Hurricane Harvey. I reside in Texas City, Texas, and work as the Adult Service Librarian at the Helen Hall Library in League City. I remember Hurricane Carla and Alicia, but they were nothing quite like Harvey. I was not prepared for what Harvey had in store.

It was early Sunday morning of August 27 when the flooding started, around 2:00 am, but the alerts and alarms had been going off all night long. So there was really no way to get any sleep Saturday night.

I live alone and was told by Emergency Management to shelter in place. I did as I was told and did not expect water to come into my home. But once it started flooding, I was basically terrorized. I couldn't see outside because the rain was constantly coming down. I first noticed a little water seeping into the side of my house and put something against the door.

Then I heard a downpour. I had no idea how or when this water would stop. When I went to the garage and opened the door into the garage, the water came rushing in. That is when I decided I should go to the attic. I did not open the garage door to the outside. Had I done that, even more water would have come in.

So I prepared to go to the attic. While I store things up there, I had never actually been in my attic. However, I was prepared to go in case I needed to.

But, of course, I was not thinking straight. I did not have a saw, hatchet or ax or anything to cut my way out of the attic. I did get my bedspread up to the attic, along with my pillow, some crackers and Gatorade. I had no idea where or when this water would stop.

After preparing the attic, I laid down on my bed because it was still dry. I did call people. My sisters live nearby so I called them. I called the city offices. I called Emergency Management. I called my councilman about a possible rescue. I was in a daze.

I cannot remember when the water receded out of the house. Did it stay 30 minutes? Did it stay an hour? I have no idea. I often think about that and wonder why I don't remember when it went back out. The water probably did not stay in my house that long, but it was long enough to terrorize me. The insurance adjuster said I got five to six inches of water in the house and eight to ten in the garage.

I only got water in the house on the first night. Many people got water when the second band of rain came through, but I did not. The water did not sit in my house for days, but I have carpet, so it is hard to tell if and when the water went out.

I stayed in my house till about noon on Sunday. Then I went to stay with a 95-year-old family friend whose house had not flooded. Her daughters and I grew up together, and she was a good friend. She knew my parents, so I went to stay with her. I never had to have someone come rescue me.

On Monday, we came back to the house and started pulling things out. My brother, who lives in Baytown, had to be rescued, but I was okay here.

I began to think of all the calls I would need to make on Monday morning to report the damage. I figured I needed to wait for normal business hours. But someone told me I could call right away. I had all the insurance information, so I called and made my case. The insurance adjusters were out to my house the next week.

Many homes were torn up for months like this one, drying out and waiting for contractors -- and supplies -- to put it back together again. This is Chris Barden's house in Friendswood.
Photo courtesy of Patricia Vance

I thought FEMA would help me but insurance only puts it back the way it was, they don't allow for improvements. So it is a vicious cycle.

By the end of September, I still didn't have floors. The contractors said I might get my floors put back in the next two weeks. Maybe.

Oh boy! Dealing with contractors: They did not ask outright how much insurance I was getting, but asked me what I wanted fixed, then offered to give me a percentage back. I just did not feel comfortable with the 25 to 30 contractors I talked with. I finally got my cousin to help me, so the work is being done a little here and a little there. As of this writing, I do have dry wall again, and that's a good thing.

People say that this kind of flood will not happen again, but we don't know that. We just don't know. So many people rushed to get their walls replaced but didn't wait for the studs inside the walls to dry. I am just reluctant to move that fast on these things.

I have always lived near the water, but never experienced it coming into my home before. As much as this was a traumatic experience, this is where I grew up.... And I guess this is where I am going to stay.

www.ingramcontent.com/pod-product-compliance
Lightning Source LLC
Chambersburg PA
CBHW070808300326
41914CB00078B/1905/J

.